Living Our Times

Living Our Times

Marie Murray

Gill & Macmillan

Gill & Macmillan Ltd
Hume Avenue
Park West
Dublin 12
with associated companies throughout the world
www.gillmacmillan.ie
© Marie Murray 2007
978 07171 3791 6

Index compiled by Cover to Cover
Design by Anú Design, Tara
Print origination in Ireland by Carole Lynch
Printed and bound by MPG Books, Cornwall

*The paper used in this book is made from the wood pulp
of managed forests. For every tree felled, at least one tree is planted, thereby
renewing natural resources.*

A CIP catalogue record for this book is available
from the British Library.

1 3 5 4 2

This book is dedicated to the memory of my parents.

Contents

Emotions and Behaviours

Ethical and Social Issues

Acknowledgments

I am most grateful to *The Irish Times* for the privilege of writing in its pages. Without *The Irish Times* this book, *Living Our Times*, would not exist. I continue to appreciate the initial opportunity provided by the *Today with Pat Kenny* team in RTÉ Radio 1 where this project began. This book also allows me to acknowledge my friends and colleagues and especially the students in University College Dublin. I have been favoured with the exceptional professionalism of all at publishers Gill & Macmillan and I am conscious of the contribution made personally by Michael Gill in directing the book's publication. Finally, no endeavour has meaning without the loving support of family. You know how grateful I am.

Preface

This book has taken seven years to write. It began on the eve of this millennium and found its first expression in a weekly slot from 2000 to 2003 on the RTÉ Radio 1 flagship morning programme *Today with Pat Kenny*. For those three years, the programme brought listeners information from the academic and clinical world of psychology and provided a psychological framework for interpreting local, national and international events.

While initially the topics were selected for the programme, listeners soon began requesting that specific subjects be discussed. Phone calls, e-mails and letters provided additional feedback to the items. In this way, a collaborative venture began. We were living our times together.

In January 2004, *The Irish Times* introduced a weekly Health Supplement in its Tuesday edition of the paper, for which it invited me to write. The supplement was designed to inform readers about general and mental health issues by providing them with a range of perspectives from diverse professionals and by covering conferences and relevant research across the entire spectrum of health.

The timing of the invitation to contribute to a newspaper allowed a seamless transition from radio to writing. It meant that the topics that had engaged listeners could now be transposed into print. It also meant that many new themes previously untouched on the radio slot could be discussed. Once again, as the column progressed, e-mails and letters from readers meant that topics were often generated by readers' requests that were relevant to these times.

The title chosen, *Living Our Times,* reflects the genesis of this book and the issues of our times. Each article is self-contained. Each was written at an interval of at least a week as a radio brief or newspaper column. Each responded to life as lived. The articles may be read as separate pieces or as clusters in the categories to which they have been assigned. It is unlikely that they will be read in sequence from first to last, but will be selected by readers either for themselves or for other people at times when the reflections they contain are relevant to their lives. For together, they form the thumbprint of this time, the individuality of our collective experience and the integration of our individual lives. All thumbprints are utterly unique. Each personal experience and public event leaves a particular mark on time, the accumulation of which forms unique, historical patterns that imprint on life as lived.

The title *Living Our Times* was also chosen because it acknowledges that we have but one life to live, one lifetime in which to live it. Whether our lives are momentary or extended, they are significant. We are born into a particular time. This we share with others, with each other. We share the music of our time, the lyrics expressing the mood of each generation, forging a special intimacy amongst those who grew up in the same era, fell in love and lived their formative years to those reverberations. Educational systems shape how we learn and what we know. Economics influence our material status. Social mores shape our behaviour. Fashion styles dictate our appearance: gendered or neutral, formal or functional, a look is created that unites, distinguishes and separates generations from each other. Religious beliefs propose value systems and the possibility of transcendence to another level of living beyond our time-limited life.

But most of all, living our times unites us with our shadowy ancestors and our imaginary descendants through raw humanity, love, sex, birth, death, hunger, happiness, sorrow, kinship, isolation, loneliness, pain, fear and courage. There is the trans-generational wish for social approbation, fear of social exclusion and contempt. There is the lure of hedonism, the challenge of asceticism, the desire to achieve meaning and the perpetual pursuit of an answer to the question 'why is there something rather than nothing?' and why are we here, now, at this time, living these times?

These are not distant philosophical questions. They are the stuff of ordinary reflections on how we live our times, in this time, with others. That these thoughts occupy people became apparent over the years as the book evolved from radio discussion to newspaper column, always shaped by events as they occurred, by the feedback from listeners and readers as well as in our internal musings as we were living our lives. *Living Our Times*, therefore, is shaped by the time in which we live. It is historically determined, culturally constructed, socially shaped and influenced by the lives of others.

Life can never be lived separately from the time in which it is lived, the people with whom it is shared, the physical environment, the mental milieu and the dominant discourses of the generation. Life is lived thought by thought, emotion by emotion, event by event: personal, public, noble, gracious, crude, aspirational and creative. We are reflective. We mull and muse and mentally mooch. We think and talk, reason and ruminate and try to determine if our inner life is like the lives of other people. We try to make sense of tragedy and to recoup psychological equilibrium when we are shocked, saddened, under threat, assaulted by nature or by each other.

Being a clinical psychologist provides a theoretical framework within which to interpret the inner world and it also provides advantaged access to the thoughts of others at their times of greatest mental vulnerability and mental strength. The joy of journalism is that it provides a way of translating these experiences into words: selecting them, examining them, extending them, crafting and polishing, altering and adjusting, savouring words, sometimes playing with them and hoping that through them will come articulation of some aspects of our human experience.

The dialogue between the dual role of psychologist and journalist conjoins clinical encounter and a place to write about what seems to matter to people. I have been privileged to combine these roles. The topics covered in the book reflect life as lived, from the whimsical to the profound. We live our lives moment by moment, event by event, lifecycle stage by stage, thought by thought, hope by hope and day by day. I hope that the articles reflect that.

What do shoes, losing a pet, adoption, toddler tantrums, aunts, romance, etiquette, letter-writing, art, death, hope, post-colonialism, de-cluttering, choosing presents, the magnificence of men, lending books and packing suitcases have in common? They are how we live our times.

CHILDHOOD
AND
ADOLESCENCE

Introduction

Living these times, we are particularly anxious to understand children, to become acquainted with their world, their developmental needs, their educational requirements, their emotional experiences, their psychological processes and the cultural and family conditions necessary for their optimal development. What are the needs of the baby, the infant, the toddler, the pre-schooler, the school-going child and the adolescent?

What makes parenting so difficult is that it is an ongoing challenge, a way of relating to children as well as a set of skills in parenting them. It is a series of tasks across a succession of life-cycle stages during which everyone in the family is personally changing and life in the external world is simultaneously changing around them. And there is little reprieve from the job of parenting, for just when parents feel that they have achieved an understanding of their children, their children abandon childhood and enter adolescence, where a new set of parenting skills are required. Parenting is a life project.

Adolescence, as a life stage, poses particular challenges for family life: a stage that young people in this millennium appear to enter earlier and exit later in emotional and behavioural terms. Adolescence has also become one of the most feared developmental phases, the anticipation of which often creates the problem it predicts, for it is difficult for young people to extricate themselves from the negative ascriptions of adolescence or to behave differently to what is believed to be the behavioural norm.

The aspirations most parents have are straightforward: that their children are healthy, happy, educated, fulfilled, in good relationships with family, friends and others and reasonably well adjusted and comfortable with themselves. The questions most parents have are realistic ones: what is expected of me as a parent? What should I expect from my child? What level of freedom, monitoring, guidance, liberty, responsibility should young people have? What do I need to know, who can inform me, who can guide me and who will support me if things go wrong?

Attempts are made to answer these questions with reference to the vast and expanding literature on child and adolescent development. Indeed, in the past decades, the combined and accumulated multidisciplinary research in psychology, neurology, linguistics, sociology, education and psychiatry provide rich reserves of knowledge about the emotional, physical, language, cultural, educational and mental world of young people. But there is another layer of understanding that we, as adults, must tap into if we are to enter the worlds of young people. The following articles invite the reader into those worlds from a variety of perspectives, conjoining the issues raised by children, by adolescents and by their parents in clinical encounters with them. In this way, they may cast a light on what is exercising the energies and anxieties of families living these times.

CHILDHOOD

The experience of childhood is usually encapsulated in vivid and visceral terms, what we see, hear, taste, touch and smell. The details of these early experiences in our childhood lives remain with us forever.

At a theoretical level we categorise these experiences and perceptions of these sensations formally under separate sensate headings: visual, auditory, gustatory, tactile and olfactory capacities. Physiological psychology thus tries to explain the intricacy of the neurophysiology of our lives; our own internal wiring, the pathways to the brain, our brain and our behaviour.

But life is not theory. Life is lived. And it is, perhaps, never lived more intensely than in childhood.

This is because the child primarily approaches the world with the totality of its being rather than living in cognitively processed separate compartments. Everything is felt: totally. Young children inhabit the present with a level of intensity that the adult world forgets. Life is immediate. It is now. Life is experienced in sensate detail; it is the strength of smells, vibrancy of colours, gruffness of textures and the softness of a parent's hand brushing distress away.

Childhood is the intense eye-wrinkling, nose-turning taste of disliked foods or the heady cool of ice cream. It is the indentation on a school desk, the texture of a toy, the sweet mouldy smell of the pages of a favourite book. The picture on its cover. It is the slap of the wind on the face or its swoosh within the ear. It is the pattern on the ceiling unseen by the adult eye, the monster on the wallpaper, the movement of the imagination across the darkened room at night.

Childhood is overheard adult conversations, half-understood, totally captivating. Childhood is watching the adult world, measuring its responses, harnessing its resources and never imagining joining its large ranks, at least not for a very long, unthinkable time.

To the adult eye, childhood looks so simple, so spontaneous and so outward. But this belies its busyness. There is an inner life of intellectual intensity, collating and assembling the jigsaw of experiences into a coherent pattern. There are messages to be understood: an identity to be assembled from the comments, compliments and criticisms of the adult world. You are good, bad, witty, intelligent, funny, hardworking, stupid, lazy, the best, the worst and 'old enough to know better'.

With these cascades of communications from the adult world, an impression of selfhood, self-esteem and self-worth are formed. I am good, bad, witty, intelligent, funny, hardworking, stupid, lazy, the best, the worst and 'old enough to know better'. Or I am none of those things. These summations of adult communications to the child are not just intellectual, they are felt with every fibre of the child's being. Children believe that they are what we tell them they are.

When a child is confronted by a new experience, all of the senses may participate in a moment of delight, terror, pain or sadness. The child feels everything with everything, with all of its being. Indeed, some of the current investigations into the condition known as synaesthesia, or union of senses, where activating one sense may trigger another, suggest that babies may not have the same separation or differentiation of the senses that most adults have. They may hear colour, taste shape, smell sound and connect with every fibre of their being to every touch, to every echo and image, to each new object, person or experience they encounter.

In other words, it is conceivable that what is felt is multisensory in its experience and intensity. Is this why babies smile and kick and wave and turn and clap and scream when they are happy? Is this why babies give such agonised cries when they are in need? Is it possible that what they feel, they feel with all their senses? Many mothers watching their children explore objects, first to the mouth, then cross-eyed infant scrutiny, then shaking and 'sounding' them out, recognise that all senses are harnessed in the baby's exploration of the world.

This far exceeds the usual level of visceral response in adults, who have learned to anticipate and recognise experiences and potential events, and to process them intellectually in a way that can dilute or deflect the strength of the event.

But in childhood, the capacity for absolute immersion in the intensity of each moment means that a child may be in a state of total delight or encounter emotions of utter despair. The child may alternate between these states and experience the plunge or ascent from one state to the next. Life is lived moment by sensate moment so that in the future 'times past' will be evoked by the most minor firing of a memory. Just as in Marcel Proust's *Remembrance of Things Past*, where the involuntary memory triggered in adulthood by the taste of a morsel of Madeleine cake soaked in tea recharges vast tracts of recollection, so, too, childhood memory and sensation provide a bridge, an arc from childhood to adulthood. A smell, a touch, a colour may suddenly melt the past of childhood into the present of adulthood or the present of adulthood back in the childhood past.

The memories of childhood, therefore, are memories of detail; a chip of paint, the fragrance of Mother's perfume, the stench of cabbage, a brilliant colour, a squelchy feeling, a dazzling day, a black night, an interminable wait, a vast ocean, a long, long road, a huge mountain, an endless journey.

In the city, there is the choking clutter of adults on a busy street: gigantic shoes, thousands, rushing by, much too close. There are eye-level buttons, waistcoats, jagged zips and leather bags. The only anchor an impatient adult hand in this Gulliverian journey through the land of the giants. They are big and you are small. Childhood is as simple and as significant as that.

Childhood is the strange smell of adult hugs; whiskered aunts and tobacco-covered uncles, grannies and grandads, the suffocation of big-bosomed embraces from friends and relations. Adults, all patting your head, ruffling your hair, asking inane questions about what age you are now, what class you are in, what subjects you favour and what you want to be when you grow up. Childhood is this adult commentary, how big you have grown, how tall you are and what a great help you must be to everyone. It is witnessing adult unease with you, their amnesia for childhood, for the language of this foreign country. They revert to a few remembered questions and phrases while your existence, your presence, your growth, alerts them to the passage of time.

Childhood is rescuing animals, the open beak of a stunned bird, the marbled coldness of dead things, the cry of a trapped cat, the wagging tail of a stray dog and the chomping, chewing curiosity in the big-eyed staring cow. It is the soft fur of animals, the warm lick of a grateful dog or its reassurance and acceptance when the entire world has banished you. It is an extraordinary affinity with nature and with animals: their spirits and yours merging, both dependent and innocent in a universe that is immense. Childhood is understanding William Blake's 'thou can't not pluck a flower, lest you disturb a star', it is knowing what that means; it is being connected to the interconnection of all living things.

Childhood is preoccupation with issues of justice and injustice, where arbitrary adult judgments are unacceptable and fairness is the first principle. It is outrage at being wrongly accused. It is devastation if privileges are unequal. Bedtime must be relative to age, homework to TV, biscuits counted carefully, the meticulous measurement of liquid into a lemonade glass and the careful division of sweets and treats.

Then there is the co-conspiracy of childhood friendships, the co-construction of games, the camaraderie of gangs, armies of affiliated friends running up and down streets in pursuit of the other. There is the best friend, the first attachment outside the home, the closeness of chums, the togetherness of talking, dawdling to school, copying of homework, reconnoitring at playtime, loitering together in the brightness of each day with occasional forays into the adult world, listening, watching, observing those adults and seeking lovers to spy on in the sand dunes in the summer.

Priorities in childhood have a different shape to adult priorities. Where is the hurry to eat when there is the chapter of a book to be finished? Why should a coat be worn when you are not cold? What could be more important than finishing the game you are about to win? It cannot be 'gone back to', it cannot be 'finished another day'. And why, oh why is the future more important than the present? Fantasy fades with adulthood, but for the child there are parallel worlds that adults do not know about and refuse to understand. Worlds they cannot enter but yet can intrude upon, drawing dreamers away from them when they are at their most exciting.

Time, too, has different dimensions. Days are endless. Summers are sunny. Picnics are excursions to seasides of vast oceanic expanse and endless stretches of sand to a shimmering horizon beyond. In the midst of this is the safe family camp, identifiable by a waving parasol or a beach towel of exceptionally lurid colour. This is the safe haven, the oasis in the desert, the refuge after bravery, the warmth after the coldness of the sea. This is the territory of gritty rug, buckets and spades, spare socks and sandals, big towels and a parent to rub the goose pimples away from the teeth-chattering blueness of Irish holiday swims. This is soggy, sand-coated sandwiches with the plastic taste of weak, warm tea and the trudge to the car for the journey home. It is too many children piled in the back and the sweaty, squashed journey pierced by bony elbows and knees while legs and thighs redden and adhere to the clammy car seats.

Time in school, also moves at a pace distinguished by the light and sounds of a classroom, chanting of letters, incantations of tables, contours of crayons making their slow squiggly journey across a page, the tongue-twisting, sniffling concentration of copying, carefully, exactly, without any mistakes.

School is the supplicant bowing of heads over a passage to be read or the bobbing of transcription from the board. It is holding the too-small piece of chalk to write upon the too-high blackboard, and the fine rising of chalk dust loitering in a sunbeam, tickling the face or clustering on the sleeve, refusing to be beaten away.

The language of childhood is the language of superlatives, the vocabulary of extremes that convey the shape of childhood experience. Unfortunately, the experiences of children are not always superlative. Somewhere in the many tasks of childhood, some children can be lost. This is because despite the many commonalities of childhood, each child lives out his or her individual, unique and special life differently and within different family, school and social structures. Working out what life is, what living is, what place you have with others, in the family, at school, with friends, with learning, with the future; these are big tasks for little people.

Those who work with children re-enter the citadel of childhood and the individual world of the child. Therapists who work with children know that they must do so with absolute respect and from a position of seeking to understand rather than to impose standard solutions. Therapists recognise the commonalities in the experiences that children have but also the multiplicity of childhoods, in addition to the multidimensional embodiment of those experiences. Each childhood is different yet recognisable. Work is with the child. It is at the pace of the child.

In order to enter, as a therapist, into the realms of childhood, one must respectfully request access to this world. The therapist then waits to be invited by the child to do so, being mindful of children's superior knowledge about their own domain. When the therapist speaks in this smaller world, then the voice must be softer, the solution must be shorter, and everything must be different because children are more fragile than adults in every way.

The therapist is prepared to follow the many delicate paths through which a child may wish to direct them before together reaching the points of mutual concern. These paths are important because they are the child's preferred routes to the problem. Sometimes they are the child's only way to reach the problem. Therapists must know that they do not know the best route to go and stomping through this small domain can cause a great deal of destruction. Better for the child to identify the path and lead the way.

But therapists do not enter other worlds without magic wands: wands made of memories, questions, empathy, common sense, sense of humour, humility, expertise, knowledge, compassion, concern, clinical carefulness and careful commitment and the capacity to work with the child and his or her parents.

DRAWING OUT
EMOTIONS

'Art does not reproduce what is visible, it makes things visible.'

Swiss Painter and engraver Paul Klee

Children love to draw. Adults love their drawings. Visible expressions of the infant mind, children's drawings inscribe themselves upon the page and the parental heart in a special way.

To the outside observer a child's drawing may appear to be no more than random marks across a page, but to the parental eye it is self-portraiture of the most exquisite kind. For it depicts what is real and relevant in that child's life and demonstrates more powerfully than words the relationship between the child and family members from the child's perspective.

This quest for self-expression begins when the infant discovers that he or she is the actual source of that visible scribble. There follows another. Another mark is made and then one more before another and another. It must have been thus with our ancestors when time began, marking out the entrance to their caves, the outline of the world beyond their shelter, maps of hunting grounds, animals to be avoided, dangers overcome, foods acquired, emotions to be recorded and depictions of their kith and kin and all those people they held dear adorning the space they regarded as home.

So, too, a child's scribble is more than a scrawl. But that scrawl is the beginning of a process of inscribing his or her individuality upon the world. Thereafter the child's arm swings to and fro and up and down across the page in the intense excitement of discovery that what is done is visible. The turn of a hand, the pressure of a finger, the choice of colour, the extension of an arm, the changes in direction appear and are controlled by one small hand engaged in the art of art itself and rediscovered by each child for the first time in his or her life. The process of self-portraiture begins. Shapes are formed. Circles appear with matchstick appendages, animated life, arms akimbo, legs splayed in disembodied dance. There are dashes for digits, collections of toes, squiggles for shoes, circles for faces, dots for eyes, triangular noses and semicircular mouths turning up or down depending on the mood. There are spikes for hair or long lines of tresses: the gender distinctions of the very young. There are freckles on faces. There are animals and trees, symmetrical houses with the people who people the world of the child.

There is concentration in the art. Lines are coloured carefully, colours chosen purposely. There are bright yellow suns and round proximate moons, many-windowed, double-fronted houses with winding paths to painted doors with numbers, knobs and bells, picket fences, chimneys with smoke spiralling up towards curly clouds and wide-winged birds skimming through the bright blue sky, deep dark oceans and mountains that are very high. All life is here if we but look. For the scrawls of childhood are more than colourful scribbles, they are the psychological palettes of the child's affective world. They are evidence of attachment, the etchings of emotion, the doodled depictions of identity and family life upon a page.

Who has not seen the 'family drawing' of matchstick men in ascending size: tall dads, long-haired mums and rows of siblings? Who has not seen 'the family' drawing with the 'new baby' absent or larger than a house or banished to the farthest corner of the page? Who upon seeing these works has not understood what place that new arrival holds in the dethroned childhood heart? How many drawings have pictures of a bullying sibling menacing the space? How many show the saddest child alone with raindrop tears forming neat lines down an elongated face? Who is tiny, who is large? How many dads are absent, committed to the side, how many mums, how many faceless partners? How many joyous, yellow, sparkling suns, how many face-sized grins, what cheerful smiles? How many tears? How many arms outstretched, how many crossed, or straight, or amputated?

The drawing of a child is the life of a child depicted in stark, salient strokes for those of us wish to understand the emotional colours that tint their inner lives. Who is drawn first? Who is crossed out? Who is not there? Who stands next to the artist and who is farthest away and why? Who holds whose hand? Who has the biggest hands, the tiniest feet? Who is looking out and who is turned away? What pets parade across the page or snuggle at the artist's feet? What landscape does the artist choose? What flowers and trees surround? What colours do their flowers have and do they droop or stand with confidence reaching upwards towards the light? What observations has this artist made about the world that we might recognise as relevant? How could such visibility ever be overlooked?

A century of studies by psychologists and educators identifies the significance of children's drawings in identifying developmental ability or difficulty, emotional security or distress, happiness or trauma and the issues that are relevant in children's lives. The therapeutic role of drawing is that it is a medium through which the child may express what it cannot verbalise, articulate what it cannot speak and visually portray what it is unable to say.

Drawing engages the senses. Children love the sight of colour, the smell of crayons, the splish of water, the scratch of pencil and the feel of bright and gooey paint. Rainbows of colours collide, crayon-deep creations adorn the house and decorate the fridge and grin from notice boards. Finger paints allow the imprint of a hand or foot and rows of vibrant palm prints bedeck the walls of nurseries and schools, followed by lively footprints of those feet that one day may imprint their power upon the world.

The gift of a drawing by a child is a gift indeed. It says to the therapist I trust you with my world. It says to the parent you are my world. Which is why no Caravaggio could replace the crumpled, multicoloured artistry of family life on crinkled paper created by a child, coloured with love, presented with pride and cherished forever in boxes of memorabilia that record the mental life of childhood and the history of mankind.

TEMPER
TANTRUMS

There is a shriek, a screech. The temper tantrum has begun. The ear-piercing, body-flinging, object-hurtling, feet-kicking, arm-flailing, hand-biting displays of the very young are utterly miserable for everyone – performers, participants and observers. For parents it is cringing in the supermarket, wrestling with a tiny tot and a bag of jellybeans, or whatever that object of desire is that has been denied, and has precipitated the toddler's tornado of rage.

The temper tantrum 'terrible twos' stage is a normal developmental stage. Tantrums, which are most common between two and four years of age, are a sign that a young child has a view on the world, has the ability to want something, has the courage to express that want, knows from whom to seek it, has the capacity to insist and has the tenacity to keep at it until it achieves what it wants or learns to cope with what it cannot have.

Having a tantrum is a sign that a child is intelligent, reaching out to learn about the world, tasting, testing, choosing and asserting his or her will. These are skills parents want a child to have, if only it wasn't so socially decimating, so decibel loud and so shattering of parental confidence, as others, observing the scene, shrug, sigh, eyebrow raise or purse their lips in unspoken belief that the child is simply 'bold' and in need of a firm parental hand.

But it is normal and appropriate that as toddlers leave baby-hood, become ambulatory, curious, exploratory and adventurous, these explorations lead them to objects that are dangerous. They do not know that plugs are not for fingers, the dog's bowl is not for licking, that the road has speeding cars, that there are things they can and cannot have or why that is so and who decides. And in a supermarket where you put what you like in your trolley, then why can't they also take what they like from the shelves? Without the use of language to explain what they want or the comprehension to understand what is allowed, the world can reduce to two words: your child screaming 'want' and you screaming 'no'.

Tantrums arise because children become frustrated, angry and upset when they cannot have what they want and do not know how to express these emotions. Sometimes they happen because a child needs attention and there is no better way to achieve that aim than a full-blown outburst at the cash desk. Tantrums often happen because a child is overtired, over the top, needs a sooth-ing cuddle, a drink of juice or a rest, or simply because they have not yet learned to understand 'no'.

Of course, some children are temperamentally more irritable, with poor frustration tolerance, so they need more help than the more compliant child. Sometimes they continue to have tantrums because they are responded to with adult outbursts of rage, of hitting and screaming that are meant to stop the tantrum but instead feed it further while modelling it as a way to behave. How parents respond to tantrums, therefore, determines the strength, length and the end of the tantrum.

The key to ending tantrums is calm, sympathetic, consistent persistence that the desired object cannot be achieved in this way so that it ceases to be a way a child tries to get what he or she desires. It is important to keep young children safe during tantrums. Holding them firmly and sympathising with their frustration is not giving in. They can hurt themselves when they are in full force, which frightens them further. Children often don't know how to stop their flood of emotions and need a calm adult to help them do so.

And there are well-tried strategies that work with tantrums, such as not to shout, slap or show a furious face when it is happening, for this frightens children, feeds the tantrum and is confusing to them. Tantrum time is not the time for major explanations that children are too out of control to hear. Never give in to the demand because that teaches the child that anger is the way to get what one wants. Don't listen to the disapproval of other people as you handle a tantrum in a gentle and determined way: your child needs understanding and protection during a tantrum, not collective adult anger against it.

If the tantrum is in a crowded place it is best, if possible, to take the child away, gently, to where it is quieter and less crowded. Helping children to name their emotions – happy, sad, cross – means that they do not have to vent them so volubly. When a child finally ends a tantrum, he or she should be praised for regaining control. Also praise a child who shows restraint in a place in which he or she previously threw a tantrum. Reward for good behaviour works better than just punishment for bad and it is good to catch children out behaving well!

Tantrums are prevented by knowing the triggers that precipitate them and by avoiding the situations in which they are likely to happen; by ensuring that you are sufficiently resourced yourself so that you can meet the needs of your young child calmly; or by getting help if you feel unable to do so. Finally, do not overwhelm children with too many toys and activities that make them so over- stimulated that they can't cope with any of them. Having to wait sometimes for treats is good training in self-control. Finally, if you think that your child's tantrums are different to others, or that there might be any medical cause, visit your GP or paediatrician for advice.

Tantrums are terrible, but think how you would feel if your child did not have the courage, the capacity or the curiosity to seek, to want, to assert and to insist on something.

It's Time
to Talk

If you are of a certain age, you will remember your anticipation of 'the talk' and 'the book'. These consisted of the embarrassed, incoherent mumblings of your same-sex parent about the 'facts of life'. Monologue completed, you were then presented with a book of minute apologetic print that contained a hybrid of medical and theological incomprehensibility, ostensibly your guide to sex.

The talk was unheard, the book unreadable, but the message was clear: don't do it. With your mortal body and your immortal soul at risk, this admonition removed ambivalence, liberated adolescents from sexual pressure and from participating in what they were not emotionally ready to engage in. The 'talk' was brief, peremptory and useful – then.

Today, there is equal implicit understanding between parents and adolescents that the sexual behaviour of either is not for explicit discussion with the other. Most adolescents recoil at the mere mention that their parents could have engaged in sexual activity other than on the single occasion required for their personal conception.

That service to humanity having been rendered, they believe that their parents are best deployed devoting their energies to ensuring their offspring are kept in the lifestyle to which they believe they are entitled. In return, adolescents shield their parents from the reality of the sexualised world in which they live and the range of culturally provided sexual seductions into which they are constantly invited by market forces.

Besides, because many parents still find talking to their children about sex exceptionally difficult, by the time they eventually share the 'facts of life', adolescents are often more sexually knowledgeable than parents are, with a stunning vocabulary of sexual savvy.

And with acute adolescent intuition, young people do not reveal to their parents what they know, how they acquired this knowledge and just how young they were when 'adult' TV, films, lyrics and magazines provided their first powerful perspective on sex. Feigned innocence is best and parental gullibility validates the time-worn adolescent adage that 'the less parents know, the better'. Parents are worried enough. No need to stress them further with reality.

It is therefore with infinite regard for parental sensibilities that sons permit their fathers to sweat and stress their way through the singular time-honoured heart to heart, man to man, father-son, birds and bees exposé. By implicit complicity between father and son, neither will burden the other with further discussion and both will reassure 'the mother' that the encounter was informative, productive and comprehensive.

Daughters receive more intermittent instruction, usually of the cautionary kind, with euphemistic reminders about being careful and not getting into trouble. And many parents, if adolescence passes without adolescent pregnancy, are content that they have fulfilled their duty to their children, whose moral and behavioural decisions in adulthood are now their own.

But is this enough? With the age of first engagement in sexual activity ever decreasing, with the incidence of sexually transmitted disease ever increasing, with a society ever dissociating sex from relationship, relationship from commitment, commitment from consequences and performance from love, there is much more to know about sex and sexuality than the anatomy of an act.

With what used to be termed 'the one-night stand' transformed into an occurrence that may take place on more than one occasion, with more than one person in one night outside a teenage dance venue, is it not time to be aware of and protect young people from these callous couplings? With sexual exchange preceding exchange of names and with social life conducted for many young people through a haze of alcohol or other substances, the traditional talk with teenagers is as outdated and useless as the quill and ink for email.

Dialogue from the earliest age is now required to provide an information source more worthy to shape our children's gender identity, body image, self-worth, behavioural repertoire, sexual understanding and lifelong ambitions than Bebo, adult movies, MTV, YouTube and Internet porn to which adolescents often report unrestricted access.

To love is to challenge, respect and protect. If we truly love young people, we need to challenge what they hear, restrict what they see, denounce what degrades them, deplore what diminishes them and promote what inspires them. We need to know what they know, understand what assails them, respect what concerns them and truly guide them.

The research is clear: young people who enjoy ongoing, warm, affirmative discussion with parents about their worth and potential, who have clear authoritative (not authoritarian) behavioural boundaries drawn for them and reinforced, who are not deprived by excess and who, when necessary, experience the love enshrined in the simple word NO are at least risk from anxiety, anger, alcohol abuse, sexual exploitation and depression.

It's time to talk.

Teens Between:
When Parents
Separate

Parents may regard separation and divorce as the solution to their problems. Their children rarely agree. Few are the children who welcome it. Many are the children who are deeply distressed.

Additionally, the desire to divorce is seldom equal amongst partners, so that the parent who neither sought nor wished the marriage to end may feel angry and betrayed by the process. Children are usually aware of this, regardless of what they are told.

An amazingly high proportion of children harbour a hidden belief that something they either did or did not do contributed to the family 'downfall'. This secret guilt imposes an inappropriate burden on children who may spend their childhood trying to accommodate their parents' new arrangements without due regard to their own needs.

Conversely, other children may work to sabotage every effort at 'successful' separation, in the vain hope that if they are sufficiently disorderly and distressed their parents may be forced to reunite, if only to deal with their disruption. Sadly, there are too many instances where the only person sabotaged is the young person, who finds him or herself in trouble in every sphere.

Separation is not a single incident, but a series of events. It is a family process that imposes change and intrudes into every corner of family life. For adolescents it can be particularly difficult because adolescence is already a time of immense change and sufficiently stressful transitional tasks without the additional burden of the almost inevitable parental acrimony that accompanies parental separation.

Adolescence is the time when young people are meant to begin their traditional process of separation and individuation on the road to greater independence from parents. It is adolescents who are meant to reduce the intensity of their childhood relationships with family as they forge additional relationships outside the home with peers and the wider community. At a metaphorical level, they are meant to 'leave' parents: it is not in their script that parents leave them.

Adolescence is the time when young people are traditionally and appropriately preoccupied with themselves: their appearance, their attractiveness, their popularity, their physical prowess, their social skills, their peer ratings, their ideas about sexuality, their vocational possibilities, their future, their happiness, their mental resilience and their own present lives. It is not a time when they are able to take on the burden of parents in conflict, of disruption in their parents' world, new parental partners with implied parental sexuality and worries about whether or not their parents are happy and able to cope.

It is because so much happens when parents separate that the immediate and long-term impact of separation on children and adolescents has been the subject of intense research, particularly since the seminal Wallerstein and Kelly investigations in the 1970s.

Clinical research findings also emphasise the unparalleled stress and psychological pain experienced by young adolescents when their parents separate. Emotional reactions may include shock, fear, self-blame, anger, anxiety, sadness and grief. Behavioural reactions may include unruly outbursts, or alternatively, age-inappropriate compliant and quiet behaviour. There is an increased risk of use of substances to dull the emotional pain.

Academic work and concentration may become more difficult as young people worry about what will happen in the future, if there will be enough money, if they will have to move house or school, whether to invite friends home or hide their new family status, if their expectations for future opportunities are now altered by scarce resources and how they will tell their school friends and teachers that their parents have 'split'.

Tension in extended family relationships is not unusual and loss of contact with special aunts, uncles or grandparents can occur. Occasions for family celebration can become complicated convoluted challenges to family diplomacy: Christmas, Easter, birthdays, Mother's Day, Father's Day, school events, sports days, debs, exams and graduations; traditional times of family togetherness can become conspicuously separate celebrations.

Some adolescents cope by distancing themselves from family, keeping busy with activities and friends, denying the significance of the changes or that they have any direct emotional impact on them. Others may react with acute sadness and mourning or resent being caught in the middle between parents' conflicts and their own conflicting loyalties to each parent.

Many young people grieve the absence of the 'departed' parent, particularly if the time spent with that parent becomes uncertain, limited or infrequent. Others, for whom fifty/fifty living arrangements are made, may equally resent the division of their world into two homes and two styles of parenting, particularly if reports of life with 'the other parent' are expected on their return from either dwelling.

A common adolescent reaction to parental separation is to become excessively concerned about the health and welfare of the parent who is the primary caretaker, especially if that parent seems to be financially or practically unsupported in the new arrangement. In instances where there is any perceived abandonment by the parent who leaves the family home, excessive anxiety is experienced about the possibility of the remaining parent also departing, because of anger, inability to cope or physical illness. For if one parent can 'abandon' you, then so can two.

One of the more catastrophic losses to security occurs if the family home has to be sold. This is loss of the location of childhood. It erases the emotional evidence of the time and place prior to family change; severs the security of familiar surroundings and removes young people from the one concrete constancy that seemed to be possible during this time of considerable change.

But perhaps the most difficult adjustment expressed by adolescents is to new relationships formed by their parents. Embarrassed by parents' more visible sexuality now that their parents are 'single' again, adolescents usually resent the presence of any new partner in their parents' lives, especially in the early stages of separation.

They may begrudge sharing their parent's time with another person, perceive that person to be the source of parental defection from the home, resent attention being 'squandered' on someone they believe to be a family intruder or fear the hurt one parent will experience if they hear of a new partner in the other parent's life.

Most of all, young people fear how they will cope with the stress of being 'teens between' parents.

HYPERPARENTING

---

*'Full many a gem of purest ray serene the dark unfath-
omed caves of ocean bear, full many a flower is born to
blush unseen and waste its sweetness on the desert air.'*
                                                Thomas Gray

Each new opportunity is a new possibility. Talents may
go undiscovered if given no medium. Inspiration and
implements are necessary. By not encouraging children to try new
activities, gifts that might later be enjoyed by the world may be
missed: gems of genius buried forever. Think of young Mozart
without a piano, Picasso without his paints. Art requires expression. Nature needs to be nurtured.

It is for this reason – to ensure that their children achieve their
potential – that parents provide as many learning opportunities
and tools as possible. They purchase paper and pens, the chem-
istry set, telescope, calculator, computer, dancing shoes, football
boots, violin, tennis racket, ice skates, skis and skateboards. They
know the possibilities in a packet of seeds and a patch of earth on
which to grow them: they know that an interest developed early

in life may provide a lifelong interest, formal hobby or livelihood in the future.

Parents know what palette, brush and paints may produce: that the etching of today may be the edifice of tomorrow and that what a child sculpts in clay this day may influence forever the adult artist that child could become. They know that each activity may unlock a lifelong interest or career for children. You cannot cross the ocean if you never see the sea.

Autobiographies often reflect the importance of early intervention: the writers whose homes held tomes of literary magic to captivate and enthral a child's imagination; the musicians whose lullabies were melodious notes practised, played or sung in homes effused with tune. Former Wimbledon Women's Champion, Venus Williams, in whose baby hands a tennis racket was placed, could not have succeeded without her parents' sacrifices. Opportunities matter. They have to be given.

But in the wish to unlock potential through activity there is also the danger of locking away one of the most important lifelong skills: that is, the capacity for solitude, for silence, the ability to be still. This is not just the chance 'to do', but the opportunity 'to be'. If activities become all consuming there is insufficient time to process information, practise what has been learned and concentrate on preferred occupations.

There is merit in spending time that is not adult organised, in activities that are not goal oriented, in occupations that are not competitive and in unscheduled time alone or in the company of friends. Too much parenting is hyperparenting. It may be counterproductive, racing a child past his or her potential talents because of the speed of exposure to possibilities and overexposure to them.

So prevalent is the practice of ferrying offspring by car from one learning context to the next that this mode of parenting has acquired the title 'hyperparenting'. Hyperparenting is parenting that privileges constant activity: intensely competitive sport, simultaneous engagement with diverse skills, additional academic tuition or endless extracurricular classes. Too many activities may thwart that which parents originally set out to achieve and convey negative messages to children, whose childhood memories may consist of car drives observing the back of their parents' heads.

Hyperparenting may begin at birth with overzealous provision of developmental aids. Hyperparenting may imply to children that they are valued for their achievements more than for themselves. It may encourage the mentality that only measurably productive time has merit. Since few children can excel equally well at everything, there are inevitable experiences of failure and activities for which a child has neither inclination nor ability. There may be conflicts between ballet and karate, calculus and cookery, football and flower arranging that may strain body and brain with dissonant demands.

Hyperparenting can overwhelm children educationally, exclude them socially and discourage them emotionally. Children who are timetabled are unable to structure their time. Childhood is not for the creation of CVs or extensive social networks. Young children need time to form good friendships, initially with a small circle of friends. Being competent with confusing clusters of children may provide some social skill but might equally engender emotional or social superficiality. Friendships grow with contact in a different way to the relationship with acquaintances.

The capacities to be still, to amuse oneself, to observe, question, discover, process and reflect are crucial competencies. They are not taught. They are not contrived. They are allowed. They happen. The child who, in addition to some educational opportunities, has time to 'stop and stare', to daydream and to imagine is truly fortunate.

Moments of invention often occur in solitude. Isaac Newton had time to sit under a tree, look up at the sky and down on the earth. He had time to see an apple fall and to question as it fell down why that should be, why it should fall in that direction and not upwards, why things fall at all. Solutions find space during stress-free times, as Archimedes discovered relaxing in his bath. Germination is the generator of genius. How can it happen for children if too many seeds are sown and they have no space or time to grow?

Summer schedules can enrich the education of children and there are wonderful activities of which they can avail. But gentle time with a parent is also important and it is often what is recalled later in adult life. It is what matters amongst one's memories. It is what is recounted when someone tries to communicate to another person the important essence of the relationship with a parent in the past.

It is therefore significant that amongst the memories of Seamus Heaney in his poem 'Clearances' is his specific memory of a time he shared as a child with his mother. This was, he says, 'when all the others were away at Mass' and he was 'all hers' as they peeled potatoes. The image is of mother and son at the sink, the splish of the water as the potato skins they were peeling dropped down and the simplicity of that shared activity that seems to have been about togetherness rather than goals.

At her deathbed, this is the time with her that he recalls most vividly from his childhood life with her, during which activity they were, as he puts it, 'never closer the whole rest of our lives'.

And we understand what he meant by that.

GENERATION
STRESS

The Death of Childhood. Childhood Contaminated. Generation Stressed. Toxic Childhood. Junk Culture. These descriptions of childhood as robbed, eroded, tainted and invaded in the twenty-first century headlined the great debate that erupted in Britain in 2006 when 110 leading paediatricians, psychiatrists, psychologists, teachers, academics and authors posted an open letter in the *Daily Telegraph*. The letter called on the British government and the general public to understand the realities and subtleties of child development.

The signatories to the letter read like the Who's Who of British expertise, with heavyweights such as Sir Richard Bowlby, Dr Penelope Leach, Dr Dorothy Rowe and Professor David Pilgrim amongst them. What they say cannot be sidelined as the isolated perspective of one professional, uncorroborated, aberrant, clinically unsubstantiated or academically uninformed. It may not be palatable, but it is impressive. Their letter cannot be ignored.

Expressing concern at the escalating incidence of childhood depression and children's behavioural and developmental conditions, the letter warns that society seems to have lost sight of children's emotional and social needs. It has become clear to the signatories 'that the mental health of an unacceptable number of children is being unnecessarily compromised and this is almost certainly a key factor in the rise of substance abuse, violence and self-harm amongst young people'.

The letter identifies a number of negatives in children's lives. One key problem they cite is the impact of technology on the developing brain, 'which is not able to adjust, as full-grown adults can, to the effects of ever more rapid technological and cultural change'. They express concern about the way in which children are 'pushed by market forces to act and dress like mini-adults'. They specifically identify the unsuitability of the electronic media material to which children are exposed.

Children, they say, need what developing human beings have always needed. They need life to be real. They need real food, real play and real adults: not junk food, sedentary screen-based entertainment and absent adults. Children need 'first-hand experience of the world they live in and regular interaction with real-life significant adults in their lives'. Children also need time. They need protection from stress. The authors point out how children 'in a fast-moving hyper-competitive culture are expected to cope with an ever earlier start to formal schoolwork and an overly academic test-driven primary curriculum'.

Of course these authors acknowledge that the problem is a complex socio-cultural one with no simple solution and so they petitioned parents and policy-makers to start talking, as a matter of urgency, about ways of improving children's well-being. This is why the Hold on to Childhood campaign was launched in Britain. And it brought an avalanche of letters, commentary, condemnation, critiques and confirmation of the concerns to the debate. The talking has certainly begun.

But what about us here in Ireland? What relevance, if any, has this debate for Irish childhood? It would be easy to dismiss the concerns as those of our neighbours, not our own, were it not for the fact that responsible parents, paediatricians, psychologists, psychiatrists, teachers, child care experts and mental health professionals in this country have also been issuing warnings for a long time about the stresses on children, the erosion of innocence, the sexualisation of childhood and the influence of inappropriate media images on the heart and mind of the child. Not to mention the week the airwaves ruminate on how to control young Junior Certificate students celebrating their results with alcohol poisoning, street violence and queues for STD clinics the following day.

Parents have long been aware of the developmental need for play, the fact that children need space to initiate their own creative, imaginative, symbolic worlds, and not just be passive recipients of prefabricated fantasy. The problems of diet and obesity, anorexia and bulimia, and the increasing levels of childhood depression and adolescent ennui, angst, self-harm, suicide, unprovoked attack, substance abuse and alcohol consumption have also been articulated in this country.

But while concerns have been aired, they have not always received media persistence and have been responded to with the fleeting inattention of the soundbite: significant for a day, disposable, dispensable, replaceable. This has left parents unsupported. Clinicians, aware of how mentally unprotected childhood is and who wish that government would protect it more, are also left without sufficient sustained support for their endeavours.

Genuine concern by experienced clinicians who work with children and adolescents has often been relegated to the moral panic of cranks, the arrogance of interfering experts or the nanny-state mentality of the morally preoccupied. Real debate has been stifled by polarities, claims and counterclaims, by proponents of single causality, and the outrage of vested interests that do not want their practice of targeting child consumers to be curtailed.

Arguments about childhood have therefore become predictable. Any attempt to critique current childhood is dismissed as a retreat into a nostalgic, idealised childhood of former times that ignores the harsh realities of poverty and physical hardship that occurred then. This is unfair. Nobody would deny that health and dental benefits, educational opportunities, social and gender equality and even life span were inferior in former times to those enjoyed by children today. But there were also freedoms, mental space, time, structure, opportunities to be close to animals and nature, to use the imagination and to learn to cope with adversity.

Far from being shortened, it could be argued that childhood has actually been extended into adulthood because many young people are not being asked to grow up. What real-life challenges have they experienced to equip them to undertake adult roles? They have been cosseted and confined in perpetual immaturity and electronic hyperreality and do not know how to cope with life as lived in the real world when they encounter it. They have no time with their parents, no role models to guide them and no experience of functional family life. For the child requests no more than the adult enjoys: the sedation of substances, the salve of consumerism and constant electronic entertainment to counteract the loneliness of Western individualism and post-modern, commuter-dominated family life.

We have inverted our protections: have become physically overprotective and psychologically remiss; imagination has been colonised and entertainment has become an inane anaesthetic. We do not allow children the freedom to play, run, climb and explore outdoors, yet we allow them to enter the darkest and most dangerous mental enclaves of violent and pornographic encounters. We then express surprise when the behaviour of vulnerable minors mirrors what they have seen. This mental milieu in which they are reared is toxic to development and were it a physical pollutant there would be public protest, sustained complaint and government action.

Finally, there are many who point out that each generation has panicked about the next and that children today will adapt and emerge as badly or well adjusted as we did from the bizarre child discipline ideology of past times that saw corporal punishment as the panacea for childrearing. But we need to remember that many did not emerge unscathed from those ill-informed practices and many adults continue to struggle with mental distress inflicted by that insensitive time.

Current childhood is not harbouring the demise of civilisation. But there are practices today that will rightly outrage future generations. Amongst them will be the awful insensitivity of adults to the emotional rights of the child to protection from the mental violence of age-inappropriate media exposure that intruded into their early years, abused their innocence and packaged, marketed and sold their childhoods.

There is therefore an opportunity in our British neighbour's outpouring about the theft of childhood: to examine our own cultural conditions and what appropriate measure we might put in place to protect the mental health of children, which Irish research has also identified as problematic. This is our chance to embrace what is best in the conditions of life for children today but also to challenge what is inappropriate to their developmental needs. And this time, perhaps, we might ensure that we do not enter either/or debates that proclaim that the past was perfect and that the present is pernicious, but manage, as advised, to keep it interactive and real.

Whole World
in Their Hands?

―――――――

Parents cannot control their children's Internet use. Or so they say. So do their children. Research conducted on behalf of the Department of Justice, Equality and Law Reform and the Internet Advisory Board by Amárach Consulting found that a staggering 81 per cent of parents agree that they can neither control nor monitor their children's Internet use because, quite simply, 'they don't know enough about it'.

This gap in parents' computer competence compared to their children's confidence about media is such that the combination of parental anxiety and lack of knowledge makes this one of the most contentious issues between parents and children today. It leads to endless rows and extreme action. Parents increasingly leave for work with the coil of cables that usually connect computer to socket and port to phone as their last-resort means of keeping their children off the home PC. Young people smirk as they insert their own set of leads, access a wireless area or simply access the net somewhere else.

Parents who are more *au fait* with technology try to password protect home access, but a surprising number of children crack the code. And who needs home access when it is easily got elsewhere? Additionally, many parents are confused about the inter-action between entertainment, information and communication media. Hardly surprising, as these media increasingly merge and converge.

How, then, is one to understand more about DVDs and MP3s, about mobile phones, games consoles and their relative roles in the lives of children, their benefits and potential dangers? Who is monitoring what? Where does responsibility for child safety lie? What are the main domains in which families interact with the Internet and what is appropriate use of the Internet in home, school and out-of-home settings?

And why do parents feel so immobilised by it all? It is as if someone had pressed the pause button freezing them into in-action and suspending them in a spell of fear while around them their children are logging, blogging, browsing and texting, and generally LOL (in text parlance, laughing out loud) at the magic of media their parents do not understand.

The site of much current parental angst is Bebo (Blog Early Blog Often), advice taken by as many as half a million Irish users. Along with myspace.com, a similar site which has the added advantage of allowing users to upload their own music, these are social networking arenas that have become the new cyber social domains of the twenty-first century. But concern about Bebo is symptomatic of a wider social discourse about who controls the media and the mental, marketing, value and ethical environments children occupy.

For many parents, Bebo is just one more Internet develop-ment to keep up with because technology is ever evolving while parents pant behind, trying to keep pace with both the positive potentialities and dangerous possibilities of the latest adolescent craze. It's a continuous challenge to understand the new vocabulary, altered mentality, technological ideology and virtual reality their children inhabit.

But like it or not, their children speak that language and visit mental worlds of which their parents are unaware. They also 'chat' to their friends through the net. They download games on their phones. They know what their parents don't know. But no matter how competent they are, they don't know what their parents know. They don't know life. And they don't know the extent of the danger that awaits them, even when they are being most careful.

Children may be technologically proficient, but being able to operate a machine does not mean that you can process its content, and that is why parents' intervention is so important at this time. The prime parent rule that one knows where children are, with whom, and what is happening in their lives applies to the Internet. Children do not go out alone to unknown places. The Internet is no different.

Of course, safety strategies change as technology changes. That is a problem. For example, the classic first rule of computer use, that it occupy a communal space visible to the parental eye, becomes less protective with the increasing availability of Internet access via the mobile phone. But regardless of technological changes there are certain net-connected rules, which may be summarised as follows: be aware, be vigilant and be knowledgeable. There are a million benefits for your child in new technology, but there are a million risks from which you cannot protect them if you don't know what they are.

Research commissioned by the Internet Advisory Board, for example, shows that children visit chat rooms more than their parents think they do. An estimated 26,000 ten- to fourteen-year-old children access the Internet at their friends' homes, where they are often unsupervised and where they explore the online world more than they would alone. As many as three in ten children communicate exclusively with people they don't know and 20 per cent of children, more girls than boys, say that someone they did not know has tried to make contact with them by asking for their home address, email, surname or phone number.

Even the most careful of children are not secure. A simple statement of where you are going this weekend can inform a predatory adult of where you will be. While children may protect their own profile, they are linked to friends who may not have secured theirs, and so are accessible if those friends admit 'new friends' to the group.

So what should you as a parent do? Ask questions. Take computer courses and also get your children to teach you. Learn their games, visit sites and check the history button to see where in cyberspace they have been. Look at telephone bills to see how long your child has spent online. Mobile phone bills will alert you to the amount of text or picture messages your child is sending. Check the suitability of game titles at sites designed to assist you to do so. Set boundaries about when and where the Internet can be accessed and for how long. Check compliance. Ensure age-appropriate material is all they see. Form monitoring cohorts with other vigilant parents and don't let your child go where Internet access is unsupervised. Warn children never to give personal information or meet anyone offline. Teach them not to click on retail sites and how to ignore scams and pop-ups. Be sure the Internet is not a substitute for friends: that they are not lonely, isolated and excluded from friendship groups. Visit Bebo. View myspace.com and report any inappropriate sites you see. Finally, email and text your children regularly, just to tell them how great they are. Your good relationship with your children is the most protective factor.

Children today, they've got the whole world in their hands. Technology provides this world, one we should welcome, enjoy and employ. The benefits are enormous, with information at the touch of a button and international contact within seconds. There are mechanisms so compact we can carry them in our pockets: our phone, e-mail, supermarket, cinema, entertainment, games console, banks, encyclopaedia, newsagent, bookshop, radio and worldwide educational and research resource.

The small screen is a big window, a window on the world, a techno-cultural reality for us to master and respect, become proficient in its use, enjoy its benefits, be aware of its abuses and protective of those who are not yet able to protect themselves.

It is not to be afraid but to be aware, not to be alarmist but alert. Because there is a reality beyond cyberspace and if traumas happen to our children, we have no rewind buttons for their lives.

THE COST
OF CELEBRITY

This is the age of icons. It is the age of celebrities: a time when young stars may surface and shine in the firmament of fame. We have discovered, developed, fabricated and fashioned many young luminaries whose swift and spectacular transition from obscurity to celebrity has sent a message to all young people – you too can be famous, just wish and you will succeed.

So seductive has the possibility of fame become, that the stated career aspiration of many school children when they are asked what they wish to be when they grow up, is that they will be famous. This ambition is not accompanied by any reported accomplishment for which they would like to achieve their fame. This curious inability to identify for what talent, deed or activity fame should be awarded highlights that fame for fame's sake is the goal. The only fame we have to fear is fame itself in a culture where any notoriety will do.

But fame may bring more than anticipated when your child is launched on the celebrity circuit. And what benefits does fame in youth provide? Does it aid or arrest the normal transitional adolescent process? Does it hinder or enhance family relationships?

What new family dynamics and sibling jealousies may emerge if one child in the family achieves, overnight, serendipitous fabricated fame? How is equitable parenting enacted? And how do parents dock the pocket money of a millionaire kid or ground the child whose chauffeur is in attendance?

If, as psychoanalyst Peter Blos suggests, intrafamilial struggles during adolescence reflect unresolved childhood conflicts, how can these be resolved if adolescence is sabotaged? What are the emotional costs of fame and how can children cope with the psychological aftershock if idolisation ends with the same incomprehensible velocity with which it began?

Research from the clinical world shows that success carries stress that weaves its way into every corner of the child's life and there is no return to the childhood inhabited prior to fame. Relationships can never be what they once were, nor can others relate to the different person the child becomes. Overnight, physical appearance may be altered: hair cut, coloured or extended; clothes chosen; images created; identity erased, replaced with an adult image of adolescent marketability. The child of yesterday may look into the mirror at this new persona stunned by the glare of public demand. The yellow-brick road can be a lonely one to follow.

Many young celebrities grieve the loss of home, security and obscurity. They become victims of the fan phenomenon: that illusion of intimacy between star and fans whereby fans believe that they have the right, simply by watching the 'screen', to know the teen in a personal way. This forges a difficult dichotomy between public and private life, a strange belief by 'intimate strangers' of ownership, rights of access, entitlement to photographs, to know the details of physique, of diet, of clothes size and of family relationships and every aspect of a child's family life.

The power of this para-social interaction relies on personal information and exposure. Mother's memories may be excavated for developmental cues to stardom: family footage of childhood events produced for public consumption. Friends may betray in the most callous way, selling private photos or morsels of misinformation for personal gain.

Central to adolescence is the issue of identity. But the identity fabricated for adolescent icons may be an insensitive, marketable exploitation of innocence. Simple youthful mistakes may be publicised for posterity. Stressful, too, is the menace of being misconstrued, of an innocent act distorted, a private moment becoming public, an innocuous remark a major offence, with no right of reply other than to deny and thereby enter a conversation that seems to corroborate what the adolescent is seeking to disconfirm in a world that watches stars rise and awaits their fall.

Friendships may fade because of a new inability to engage in the old activities – a stroll around the shopping centre, a bag of chips no longer possible – the normal rating and dating of adolescence is thwarted.

And sooner or later, young 'stars' discover that fame lasts until a new idol appears; that they are only as good as their last performance; that everything they do may be edited, interpreted and decontextualised, so that what is said about them is barely recognisable to them as themselves. That if they are in love or out of love, not yet ready for love, or ill-advised in whom and how they love, that this will be revealed publicly and speculated upon.

The history of Hollywood is testimony to the fickleness of fame, particularly for its more youthful stars. Being cast in the role of a cute child brings particular challenges when adulthood arrives and cuteness disappears. Stardom has not been kind to many of its most shining lights.

Some have had their childhood or adolescence dimmed by the relentless mercenary manipulations of those who first discovered, then exploited and subsequently dropped them. Some adolescents have been sexualised, their youth subjugated on the altar of voyeuristic insatiability and marketability. Other child stars have had to suffer the indignity of a flicker of fame, abandoned when childhood appeal became adolescent awkwardness. Yet others have cracked under the strain of scrutiny, finding public speculation and the loss of privacy too high a price to pay.

Growing up in the media glare can be excruciatingly psychologically difficult. Yet for an increasing number of Irish youth, public fame and fortune has come their way. How we celebrate their success and become sensitive to their youth is significant.

Young talent needs time and space to grow, not to be plundered and depleted by overexposure before its potential has had time to unfold. If we are to be enriched by those who are genuinely gifted, then we must identify the truly talented, not manufacture fame. We must nurture those with purity of voice, power of creativity, breadth of vision, poise, penmanship, dramatic depth and deep imagining. We must guard the new custodians of true creativity, originality, ingenuity, inspiration and inventiveness.

PSYCHOLOGICAL

Introduction

Living is in the detail. It is in the insatiable need to communicate endlessly with and about each other, our propensity to gossip and the social and salacious function such communication serves.

Life is evident in the passage of time, how we mark or attempt to erase our own temporal journeys and the amusing lifelong relationship we have with our birthdays and with age.

Life is in the unexpected, and few things are as unexpected and unplanned as falling – the physical drop, that is, rather than moral decline. For falling carries psychological significance, not unconnected with issues of age and agility and the sheer indignity of downwards descent that is not self-directed.

Life is displayed in what we wear: the fashions and foibles of each era evident in the clothes we choose, the shoes we put on, the bags we carry and the suitcases we pack. For every woman knows the importance of handbags, the sensuality of shoes and the efficiency required to pack all the holiday requirements in the ridiculously small reticules that are allowed on planes these days. Nor is the male foot invulnerable to vanity or psychological meaning as men bestride the world in their purchased or custom-made shoes. There is little men do that is not noticed by women.

Life is recorded in the letters we write, the e-mails we send, the texts we compose and the journals we keep. But as technology renders the pen an historical artefact, what will happen to the passion that love letters once held?

Our body language betrays us. Our possessions often burden us. Our manners make us. And so we attempt to control what we sug-

gest when we grimace and gesture and give our inner turmoil away in the grins, sneers and leers, the complex social signals and our extensive non-verbal communicative cues.

We are identifiable as hoarders or discarders depending on whether we stash or thrash our excess possessions. We are also identifiable by the formality or informality of our manners. For if etiquette is regarded as pomposity, which in turn has become a source of comedy, then where does ordinary courtesy stand?

Life may be incomprehensible but it is recognisable in psychological ways: in what we say and convey, what we wear and discard, our relationship with age, ourselves and with each other, in the wonderful detailed eccentricities of our era and the way we live our lives in these times. The following articles tiptoe into that psychological territory.

GOSSIP

Guess what? You won't believe this! But it comes from a most reliable source. Gossip is good for you!

So say a significant number of researchers in sociology, anthropology and psychology who study the glossemes of gossip and the complexity of this most convoluted code of communication. It is credited with ensuring organisational cohesiveness, social identity and psychological belonging; the ethologists say it is the modern bonding equivalent of the group-grooming behaviour of primates.

Gossip has been described as a genetic programme, an atavistic necessity, a throwback to the time when it was essential for survival to know the whereabouts, activities, motivations and intentions of the neighbouring tribe. It was a way of asserting affiliation and kinship, cementing the crew by the things they knew, a programme for networking, information control and the establishment of hierarchies of 'those in the know'.

Gossipers are the gatekeepers of important information, the assessors of reputations and the reinforcers of shared values. Gossip blurs the lines between private and public, fact and fiction, and forces us to examine our interpretation of the world by who we are and what we say.

Corporate psychology suggests that gossip contributes to the ideological identity of the workforce, the organisational grapevine, shared 'shop talk', information exchange, formation of alliances and denigrators of competitors. And for those excluded from organisational status, gossip is a communication currency that confers conspiratorial connection between the less powerful at work.

Gossip is a power tool for the proliferation of propaganda about powerful people in society. It does this in a seductive exclusionary way that entices the reader's attention. This is typified by the rhetorical 'guess who is going out with whom', while access to the catalogue of celebrity attendance at fashionable functions conveys the impression to consumers that somehow they too were there, or if not actually there, at least privy to the secret details of the event. Additionally, the tabloids trade on the demise of deities – the idols we construct are deconstructed, scrutinised by a sentence reassuring us mere mortals when we see how the mighty have fallen and what power we have to make them fall.

From the sociological perspective, gossip is what glues communities together, the pairing and sharing of social exchange. One study suggests that gossip can decree the moral code of a community. By identifying the errors of others, it specifies the boundaries of behaviour. Gossip is often the conveyor of censure.

In examining the difference between gossip and information exchange, research shows that men and women engage equally in communication and analysis of the 'goings on' of their companions, colleagues and circle of friends. But the tone, intensity, animation and feedback are why women's conversation is referred to as gossip while men reportedly regard their activity as 'informational exchange'! But for both men and women, gossip requires a 'triad' of participants: a gossiper, an audience and a third party who is being gossiped about, all of whom must know each other.

And what about the gossip of the *Gael?* Our own Celtic tradition laid great emphasis on storytelling. Weaving itself in myth and legend, it conjured up imaginary locals of eternal youth and characters of absolute wisdom. This art form continues to the present time as a cultural value and finds expression in the artistry of day-to-day communication. The survival of the oral tradition was linked to the special status of the *seanchaí,* or storyteller, whose activity pointed to the significance of the spoken word in recounting our history, sustaining and containing our knowledge, the speaker and mediator of our culture, our identity, our selves.

But there was another 'storytelling' subculture, signified by squinting windows, twitching curtains, wagging tongues and knowing nods, raised brows, tight lips, rigid rectitude and the capacity to convey the condemnation of the community by a curl of the lip.

These were the inveterate, invidious and vindictive invigilators of the loves and lives of others, inveiglers, invaders or even inventors of intimate information for the titillation of the tribe. Indeed, it must have been from these gorgons of gossip that the traditional *seanfhocal 'Dúirt bean liom go ndúirt bean léi, gur chuala sí bean á rá'* – the classic 'she said that she said, that she heard' – became the Chinese whispers of the Celtic community.

And this is where clinical psychology parts company with anthropological explanations, sociological solutions or the benefits of corporate cohesion through gossip. This is where it recalls the lives destroyed by a lie, damaged by 'truths' best left untold; the havoc of psychological denigration and defamation; the irrevocable said that cannot be unsaid.

This is the critical factor in the 1963 play by Edward Albee, *Who's Afraid of Virginia Woolf?* It is the series of humiliating revelations and betrayed confidences with the final unfolding that one couple's beloved twenty-one-year-old son is purely imaginary – this suffering summarises the story in a sentence.

Gratuitous gossip is confessional calumny, the slander and slaughter of reputations, the death of marriages and the trauma of social exclusion. It may be the weapon of the blackmailer, the unfair apportioning of blame and shame, the burden of the bullied, the erosion of self-esteem, the origin of social phobia, the source of social isolation and depression.

It is indecent exposure of human vulnerability and frailty and too many clinicians see too many people whose lives have been wrenched by words.

Birthdays
and Age

What is most celebrated and most dreaded? What do women conceal and men rarely reveal? What do children add to and adults subtract from? Well the answer, you know, is age.

Our relationship with age is most peculiar; we add to age in childhood, fake age ID in adolescence, conceal our years in middle age and return to proud declaration once the biblical four score and ten or celebratory centennial arrives.

Between those stages, how we view the passage of time depends upon a variety of factors: our personal self-esteem, our achievements relative to our age, the degree to which the culture we live in reveres or reviles the aging process and finally, the identity we have created for ourselves, or that has been created for us, at different life stages.

Age-related judgments of us begin early, with parents comparing developments in walking, talking and toilet training. Children are also reminded to 'act their age' according to hierarchical, age-based behavioural expectations, encapsulated in the classic admonishment to the eldest in the group that 'as for you, you're old enough to know better!'

Yet despite adult expectations, children themselves long for the incremental status each birthday brings, with promises of new competencies hitherto only observed in older siblings and playmates. So special is being 'older' that the five-and-a-half-year-old (the half is critical) soon becomes the nearly six-year-old, who can then look from the lofty heights of 'elder' advantage on the lowly status of those who are 'barely' five. And to be six! What age attainment! As the verse goes, 'now that I'm six, I'm clever so clever, I think I'll stay six forever and ever'.

Yet what was once the eagerly anticipated birthday in childhood may turn into a dreaded adult event. It is rare to hear an adult boast 'I'm almost sixty'. Rather, it is 'the right side of sixty' which still permits the declaration 'I'm in my fifties'. Because if one were to analyse our convoluted relationship with age, the pivotal factor in whether or not we wish to advance, diminish or dismiss our age depends upon the meaning a society attributes to it. In an ageist society, which privileges youth, years are not glorified unless, of course, they are extreme, when some reverence is felt for those who have witnessed and survived the passage of a century.

Birthdays hold other intense psychological dimensions. They declare that this is the day that this person, this unique life began. When others remember your birthday, they commemorate your continuance. They say, through birthday gift or card, that their lives are better for your presence, and that your presence on this earth is cause for celebration. They remind us that our arrival into the world was not an individual but a social event; of the many lives that each individual influences by their presence, filling a position that is unique to each individual, altering the family configuration, adding to the number of children one's parents possess, the number of siblings one's siblings can claim, the number of nieces or nephews, cousins and grandchildren, twigs and potential branches on the family tree.

While childhood advances slowly, adulthood sprints with alarming alacrity. Birthdays mark this process: age of reason, age of consent, age of majority, the eighteenth birthday entrée into adulthood, the twenty-first birthday acceptance into the adult community, parties for the passing of the decades, markers on life's road. These are important rituals signposting our lives.

Of course we joke about birthdays. We joke most about what we fear most. This probably explains the proliferation of macabre middle-age repartee; how middle age is when your age starts to show around your middle, or when anything new you feel is a symptom. It is the time when sexual prowess jokes emerge in proportion to the perception of threat to sexual capacity and activity. It may not be a crisis, but it is a time of serious review.

We also project our past ageist prejudices upon ourselves. When we enter the birthdays of middle age we encounter an era we remember our parents living through. We remember how old they seemed (then) to be at forty, how antiquated at fifty, how ancient at seventy, in contrast to how young we now perceive ourselves to be upon arrival at those antediluvian ages. If, tragically, a parent died in middle age, then we cannot conceive of living beyond their life span. This is the birthday we do not believe we will achieve. This is to outlive one's parents in a unique way, to exceed the chronological extent of their lives, to encounter psychological territory they did not meet, to experience time they were not given.

Birthdays are complex psychological processes, not singular annual events. Birthday parties reassure children; they were wanted, they are loved. It is for this reason that every child should have at least one special, memorable birthday: a memo to adulthood, so that regardless of their memories of childhood there is one seminal celebration to shield against moments of doubt.

Birthdays are markers. In the past, mothers who were forced to relinquish their children for adoption were left to imagine, annually, how their child might be. Many adopted children recall their birthdays as days that they too wondered from whom and whence they came and why.

Parents who have lost a child grieve especially on birthdays for the years that might have been, for the milestones never now to be attained, for the life not fully lived. Mothers who miscarry often note the date their baby should have been born with sorrow for a life denied. Even more silent is post-abortion mourning, emerging in clinical conversations but otherwise suppressed.

Birthdays punctuate our lives. And as we get older it is more difficult, perhaps, to delight in the next milestone on a life path whose end is becoming more visible, whose horizon is no longer protected by the optimistic myopia of youth. This is a path whose most sensational, scenic views may lie behind, with uncertain terrain ahead. This is a path on whose sharp stones we may already have stumbled and whose steep and lonely incline seems daunting at its end. This is a journey which beloved partners and friends may have completed, leaving us to pick and trip our solitary way through its final stages, alone. This is the journey to journey's end.

But it is not yet over, whatever age you are. It is therefore important, always, to celebrate your birthday, make it a marker for what you have done last year. Make up magnificent plans for the year ahead. Without this magical thinking, birthdays are dreary days instead of marvellous possibilities.

Psychological research shows that we must dream in order to actualise our desires. Birthdays provide the perfect opportunity to do so.

FALLING

_____

Falling is not just a physical event. It has psychological dimensions. It carries emotional significance beyond the inbuilt indignity of thudding towards the ground in ungainly fashion. It shakes more than the body to find one's person unintentionally prone: the ego is dented, the security core is injured and confidence is damaged temporarily. For a fall is the first step (or rather, the loss of footing) in a series of inevitable events that follow that fall.

There is a moment during which one is walking steadily, securely, two feet planted firmly on the ground, so to speak, just before one trips, slips, collides, drops, plummets, plunges, thuds or careers outwards, downwards, backwards or sideways into uncontrollable, unpredictable nothingness. The instinct is to grasp at anything that might keep one upright and deflect the impact of the fall. There is a sickening second when it is apparent that no help is 'at hand'. Landing shakes the body, then mental shock: sight of blood, regression: hands held outstretched and the wish to howl like a child. Not until the anaesthetic of shock wears off do the other minor, niggling cuts, bruises and abrasions tingle into soreness. Truly falling is traumatic.

A fall may happen at any time, anywhere, to any person, whether alone or amongst others. Of its nature it is startling, sudden and unexpected for the faller and witnesses. It may cause superficial injury, requiring no more than the application of sympathy, antiseptic and plasters, or it may have serious physical consequences requiring emergency medical intervention and long-term recovery.

Luck is almost always involved, as to where and how one lands and the damage done in descent. The tragedy of a fatal fall is this fate dimension, particularly if the person who falls is young. In a second a confident, capable, older person who falls may become dependent and thereafter lose trust in their capacity to live safely, independently and well. Family may fuss, or alternatively may not appreciate how shaken an older person feels after what seems like a simple fall. There are psychological consequences to every fall.

There is often such a fine line between the superficial and serious injury that the thought of what might have happened is part of the shock for those who fall. The aftershock of a fall derives from the second before impact, when anything is possible. Another inch and an eye might be impaled, a limb fractured, teeth shattered, wrists cut, a nose broken. The wrong bump can cause spinal injury, the right landing can mean simple cosmetic inconvenience for a week or two. Destiny dictates. That is what shakes us if we fall, to look in the face of chance and know that it is in control. 'Rough hew it how we will' providence plays a major part in our lives.

Apart from serious falls, there are social falls, those embarrassing occurrences when the party guest trips: red wine seeping into linen, clutching the person of strangers to prevent descent. These mishaps call for the social solicitude and the reassurance of host and hostess that it could happen to anyone, while the remnants of designer glass glitters like gritted teeth from the parquet floor.

Bizarrely, people often laugh when others fall, prompting entire TV programmes to pay for home videos of people suffering the indignity of a fall. Pavement falls bring public humiliation, trying to show passers-by that you are fine by limping away with alacrity as they retrieve your scattered goods and groceries. You ignore the carrots wedged in the gutter, your gloves soggy in a puddle, clothes mud spattered and torn and hope the hotel doorman will admit you, in your dishevelled state, to use the facilities for a private weep. Falls that cause facial bruises and bumps bring suspicious glances that one has had cosmetic surgery or been the victim of domestic cruelty or insobriety, and it is the brave husband who accompanies his wife in public places in the aftermath of a fall.

There seems to be insufficient notice paid to 'falling' in psychological research, although psychoanalysis is attentive to metaphoric meaning and the 'Freudian slip'. Our language is replete with allegorical reference to physical and psychological descent. In biblical terms the misery of human life began with 'The Fall'. Evil is represented by fallen angels. Dante emphasises the pilgrim's spiralling descent into hell. History records the rise and fall of empires. We see how the mighty are fallen. The crime is solved through a slip of the tongue. Destitution is termed skid row. We trip people up when we reveal their deceit. We fall for a con, a story or a scam. We plunge into debt. Shares drop. We are out of step, off balance, on a downward spiral. In need of support or a pick-me-up, we lose our footing, lower ourselves, teeter on the brink, go over the edge and are upended. Even love is not something within our control but something we fall into. To the outside observer a small fall may look like an insignificant thing. But to those who experience it, the most minor tumble can be traumatic.

And of course, whatever your perspective on the subject, let us not fall out about it.

Putting One's
Foot in It

You would think that the shoe would be a simple shield between sole and street, defending the walker from the roughness of the road and ensuring that no dangerous objects penetrate the pedestrian. Not so. The shoe is an object of spectacular sociological data, for it encases the female foot in a way that has engaged men and women since fashion began with the fig leaf.

Psychology has paid insufficient attention to the female foot and the mental machinations that accompany its encasing. Apart from a discrete literature, focusing primarily on paraphilic fantasies including, of course, the significant shoe fetishes, little is said about the psychology of popular preoccupation with shoes that has converted covering the foot into a multimillion, multinational industry.

If fetishism involves obsessive, inappropriate love, then a peep into many women's wardrobes may provide evidence of pathology. For the shoe is not just a love object for women, it is an object that is loved. It arms (or should one say foots) the wearer daily for a wide variety of activities. It provides indices of age, occupation, interest, advantage and the knowledge of appropriate attire that the wearer displays for those cognisant with the message communicated by the style, colour, shape, serviceability, function or frivolity of the chosen pair. Shoes are social and sociological signals to those who look down on others to see what shoes they are wearing today.

There was a time when nationality was uniquely distinguished by shoes: the clogs of Holland, the beautiful Indian mojaris, the Siberian Sami shoes made of reindeer, the pampooties of the Aran Islands along with our durable brogues. Meanwhile, the Manchu women in China were notable for their New Year's Eve display of beautiful embroidered shoes, to the base of which were attached blocks to protect their delicacy from dirt. And even in present times, one can inadvertently put one's foot in it, culturally, by wearing shoes into Japanese homes rather than leaving them at the *geta-bako*, or shoe cupboard, in the entrance area as tradition in many Asian cultures requires.

What of the delicacy of the aristocratic French foot? Who knows if the anger engendered in the impoverished French peasant soul for revolution was not more about the affront of silver-buckled, jewel-encrusted feet emerging from carriages than the insensitive suggestion that the starving masses eat cake? The original Birkenstocks are to this day linked with German utilitarian orthopaedic footwear, although Doc Martens became deliberate punk protest footwear for a while. But the Italians, perhaps, have always outshone, with Italian designer Salvatore Ferragamo being one of the first to put new synthetic material to use in shoes. And who but the Italians would have provided the stiletto, the source of men's fantasies and women's most secret desires? Or consider the Renaissance Venetian chopines, sculpturesque works of art more than items of clothing. To this day the peeping toe, the slingback heel, the seductive sandal and quintessential good taste are to be found in Italian design.

Of course, climate dictates outdoor wear, and while Gene Kelly may have had a spring to his step while singing in the rain, rain is the ruination of delicately adorned feet. Yet what young woman would ever succumb to comfort and wear sensible, serviceable shoes when a figment of fabric and imagination can festoon her feet?

Why the shoe should have imprinted so scantily on psychological research is a mystery given the information shoe analysis provides into the female psyche and the 'sole' of society itself. Furthermore, research is rendered ridiculously easy in that one sitting in a high-quality department store could provide significant quantitative and qualitative shoe research results on the progress of the populace in our times.

Where would forensics be without footwear? The distinctive footprint below the privet an inevitable clue for the Miss Marples and Hercule Poirots of past popular suspense before technology made slivers of tissue more relevant to fictional thrillers. But footwear can never be aurally redundant if one considers the click-clack of heels, squeak of soles, clump of wedges and tap, tap of tiptoeing indulged in on the stairway by those who wish to keep their late arrival home a secret from either alert parental or spousal ears.

Many men are unaware that they compete for their wife's affections with Christian Dior, Manolo Blahnik and Jimmy Choo, or that SJP's lifestyle has more influence on their mate's desires than they. And when a woman starts whispering 'my Manolos myself' and changes from being sensibly shod to slipping into reptile skins, T-bars, silver sandals or 'Berties', then it's time for him to pay attention.

A psychological vocabulary surrounds the shoe. Being well-heeled hints at understated wealth, while being on one's uppers means reduced to the remnants of over-worn shoes. Putting one's foot in it, unless the 'it' is a shoe, is to be avoided, while behaving like a heel describes the basest of behaviour.

Without the right shoes, how can you put your best foot forward, be in step with the times, march out in style or, if you choose to discard your footwear, be footloose and fancy free?

It is no coincidence that the shoe has a tongue: for shoes speak to the wearer in a particular way, as they do to those who watch what others wear.

All of which begs this question: what do your shoes say about you?

Following in
Father's Footsteps

———————

Shoes are not an exclusively female fixation, for an equal, if different, psychology applies to how the male chooses to be shod. Indeed, if psychology has been inattentive to female footwear, it has been utterly neglectful of the male. Because the manner in which man 'bestrides the narrow world like a Colossus', and the footwear he requires to do so, give much information into his attitudes and aspirations in life.

The original image of the male biped is a powerful one. Man's foot unadorned, large, splayed and strong. And when he first stood up on his own two feet, he began a special skilled, species-specific journey. With hunting agility, he created his earliest shoes, fashioning the animal skins of his prey upon his feet. Since then, step by step, he has marked, measured and progressed upon this earth and beyond.

Think of the lunar landing in 1969, when Neil Armstrong, stepping out upon the surface of the moon, took 'one small step for man' and 'one giant leap for mankind'. This brings to mind the words of another man, Henry Wadsworth Longfellow, on how the lives of great men all remind us how 'we can make our lives sublime and departing leave behind us footprints on the sands of time'.

But there have been other, less noble occasions when man has put his foot down, and has marched in military stomping synchronicity to war. From the Roman sandalled centurion to the current combat boot, soldiers have been uniformly shod and sent to fight, as echoed in Rudyard Kipling's account of the Infantry Columns' 'foot-slog-slog-slog-sloggin' over Africa, boots-boots-boots-boots-movin' up an' down'.

Consider the polished killing proficiency of the brutal, black-booted Nazi machine: the abandoned shoes of tiny children in the death camps of Auschwitz or Dachau. Too many men have 'died with their boots on' and too many women have waited for the footsteps of a beloved husband or son who never made it home.

But the boot is on the other foot when it comes to fashion, whereby it becomes a wader, a Wellington or the riding boot associated with an ascendancy class to whom ill-shod men once tipped their caps in servitude. In fact, the history of footwear highlights the degree to which what one could afford to put on one's feet was often determined by wealth, rank and class. For example, in seventeenth-century France, King Louis XIV, being of short stature, wore high heels, shoes he did not permit the populace to wear, while in eighteenth-century England the low-laced, leather Oxford shoe, tied over the instep, became an Oxford don favourite and an international standard for male footwear thereafter.

But one must not neglect the many other fashions by which men's shoes define the man: the implied promiscuity of the pointy toe, the sensual empathy of rounded shoes, the dominance of the durable heel, the dandyism of men who chose dainty wear, while even today the cowboy boot remains beloved of women when worn by their men. The 1920s saw the Gatsby-style two-tone spectator shoe, the winklepickers of the 1950s are memorable, and who could forget Elvis Presley's gyrating musical injunction that you do anything to him but step on his blue suede shoes.

Nor has art neglected men's boots and shoes, given the vibrancy of Vincent Van Gogh's *A Pair of Boots* and Andy Warhol's *Shoes, Shoes, Shoes* to name but two. Religion recognises shoe symbols: washing and anointing of feet, fitness to tie a lace, the shoes of the fisherman, the monastic sandal, a father's provision of footwear for his prodigal son and the miracle of He who walked upon the earth and sea. When entering Buddhist monasteries and Muslim mosques, men leave their shoes outside to keep the inside clean for prayer.

Sigmund Freud, inevitably, found something fetish-like and phallic in feet and shoes, but he is not alone in seeing their analytic significance. For it is with his feet that man touches the earth and the psychological power behind the Irish male brogue is immortalised in poem and play and tale.

Consider the lonely boots on the empty stage in Samuel Beckett's *Waiting for Godot* and how Estragon and Vladimir subsequently discover that trying on boots can 'pass the time' and be 'an occupation, a recreation, a relaxation'. Uncle Manus's brown shoes with worn-down heels appear in Seamus Deane's novel *Reading in the Dark*. Poet Máirtín Ó Direáin commemorates the purchase of a child's first pair of shoes, reflecting upon all the steps those feet will take thereafter. Seamus Heaney's 'Blackberry Picking' tells how 'briars scratched and wet grass bleached our boots'. And no account of men's boots could omit Heaney's tributes to his father's work, ploughing and digging, while he, a child, followed him, stumbling 'in his hob-nailed wake' or watching as 'the coarse boot nestled on the lug'.

Surely grief must be an empty shoe in which a man will walk no more.

Shoes have a sturdy psychological significance for men, binding them to one another, fathers beside sons, standing firmly together on terra firma. There is a gift bestowed or a burden placed upon men who must follow in their father's footsteps.

But if men must walk a distance in their father's shoes, with what care must fathers tread, what steps must fathers take for their sons to follow?

The Importance

of a

Handbag

Handbags are important. Anyone of sufficiently advanced age and good fortune to have seen the late Micheál MacLiammóir at the Gate Theatre play Lady Bracknell, or more recently to have witnessed Alan Stanford bring that good lady to life in the Abbey Theatre, will know the importance of a handbag. For the handbag is central to the plot and final denouement in Oscar Wilde's *The Importance of Being Earnest*. The play portrays, as never before, the importance of a handbag in terms of owner and occupier identity.

For this reason, a case may be made for more earnest psychological attention to the handbag as the site for assessment of owner idiosyncrasies. Handbags also provide psychological insight into their owners' organisational capacity. Simply ask for some everyday object and observe what emerges from the bag. Retrieval versus rummaging is the key.

Research should commence with women's handbags. For while men and women have carried their belongings since they had belongings to carry, women's handbags have cultural significance warranting investigation. Handbags are private and personal. Analyse the handbag and you analyse the woman. Whether custom made or mass-produced, once acquired, the chosen handbag incorporates the public persona and secret life of its owner.

The type, colour, shape, fabric, decoration, individuality, flippancy or functionality of a woman's handbag provides crucial cues to the character of the holder. And while its external appearance, age, quality and purpose yield some information, it is upon examination of the inside of the bag that the potential for more penetrating psychological analysis of the handbag owner resides.

The choice of contents, their number, purpose, location, organisation and accessibility are a revelation. Consider the efficient bag owner who can extract any required object immediately upon request. This is the person who can remove her mobile phone on the first ring, whose diary appears like magic at the suggestion of a meeting, who always has accessible pen and paper, who, with one quick wrist flick, produces a tissue for those who sneeze, a bandage for the unexpected cut, a silent lozenge for those who cough at the concert hall and a compact umbrella at the first raindrop.

She will always have the correct coins for bus, toll or parking meter. Her ticket will not be lost, nor will it emerge with sticky postal stamps, lipstick daubed and make-up tainted from the bowels of her bag. Locating car keys does not require ungainly pounding of her person in the hope of a jingle. Hall door keys are ready so that shopping need not sit in puddles on the doorstep. Routine rummages in the depths of a disorganised handbag are not required. Her office keys are never left at home and her family does not engage in daily hunts for her handbag.

The organised handbag person is someone whose business card, passport and boarding card are available in neat wallets, while her opposite number dives into a handbag the size of a suitcase in which nothing can be found amongst the clutter, the detritus of days, yesterday's sandwich, last Christmas's gift-tokens and the note her child has forgotten to give the teacher for five consecutive days.

While women often have one favourite handbag, few women confine themselves to one bag. Handbags may be fashionable or functional, stern or stylish, elaborately embroidered works of art, ergonomically efficient, designer driven, ridiculous reticules or perfectly practical hardwearing specimens for everyday wear. They may be classic or ethnic, day or evening, outfit matching or clashing, with clasps, fasteners and buckles that click, snap, tie or zip.

Handbags may be circular, rectangular, oval, chunky, elongated, chic, simple, understated, sequinned or ornately adorned. They may be metallic, bronze, gold, silver or copper, mono or multicoloured and have handles, shoulder straps or none. They may be carried, clutched, held with panache or worn with grace. They may be crafted, carved, knitted, woven or sewn, of silk and softest leather or cheap and cheerful straw. They are more than accessories. They are life companions so that a woman without her handbag feels bereft.

Lady Bracknell had it wrong when she said that 'to be born, or at any rate bred, in a handbag, displayed a contempt for the ordinary decencies of family life'. Because the handbag is an integral part of family life.

Children mimicking mummy still portray 'ladies' by gender markers: the click-clack of high heels and the carrying of handbags. And every child knows that from a mother's handbag come miracles: cotton for cut knees, cents for sweets, combs for tangled hair, wipes for noses, drinks for dry throats, a remedy for each exigency in a child's life.

While at the bottom of the bag lie the secrets of womanhood: sweet-smelling perfume, magical compacts with miniscule mirrors, scissors and shiny lipsticks, mobile phones, notebooks with joined writing, envelopes with mysterious contents, unidentifiable objects and money for everything. One never knows what treasures a handbag may contain.

A handbag! Mothers' handbags contain memories. Memories of childhood emerge at the sight of that handbag, memories bred and forevermore connected to that handbag.

Whether it had handles or not!

PACKING IT
ALL IN

There is an art to packing a suitcase. An art only some people possess. In fact, possessions are the plague of packers because there is so much to choose from.

Those that insist on bringing all their belongings with them inflict excess stress and struggle on themselves, and others, before they finally lug their battered bags and dislocated vertebrae back home.

But it is not just their own bones that are out of joint, so too is the humour of their fellow travellers, who, having packed light, find themselves carrying incongruous carrier bags, into which their over-packed travelling partner has stuffed the final belongings that not even sitting on the suitcase could crush. Indeed, research might well find that the high proportions of friendships that fracture on holidays do so because of what their friends pack, rather than any specific personality clash.

For packing does not end when the humongous holdall has been heaved through the hotel door. It spills its entrails around shared bedrooms, bathrooms and balconies for the rest of the holiday 'break'. And determined to justify bringing such detritus in the first place, over-packers delay everyone daily as they decide which of their very many, unnecessary outfits they will wear today.

Holiday packing can threaten relationships. There are men who believe that women take wicked delight in making them lift, lug, heave, heft and carry suitcases containing the proverbial 'kitchen sink' as a proof of their manhood, their dedication and devotion to them and as a means of warning other would-be women prey that they are already 'bagged'.

Some men also maintain that their wives punish marital misdemeanours by adding additional kilograms to their holiday kit. But whether this suspicion of surreptitious revenge is valid, or whether this is the paranoia of the philandering male, has yet to be proved.

Perhaps this is why in pre-modern times travelling men travelled alone. Who could imagine Odysseus trundling a whining wheelie as he made his way home to Penelope, his wife? And surely Anthony and Cleopatra would never have fallen in love if he had been forced to transport all the milk and honey for her evening ablutions everywhere they went. Aphrodite would never have risen from the waves if she had to deliberate over which bikini to wear, and how could Cupid fly to so many hearts if he had to clutch more than his bow and arrow wherever he went?

This is not to belittle the topic of baggage. Nor is the psychology of 'packing' a subject unworthy of study. A 'case' can be made for the diagnostic potential of distinguishing the deft traveller from the disastrous trudger, simply by observing who claims what suitcases as they make their battered rounds of the carousel. For much is revealed about us as people, depending on how and what we pack, when we pack, in what kind of suitcase, to which destinations, for what purpose, with whom we travel, with what frequency and for what duration, not to mention what we do and where we go while there.

Light packers who pack all that they need and no more than they use challenge fellow travellers every step of the way. They neither sweat nor stumble, they do not push recalcitrant trolleys, trundle suitcases, crouch over cascading case contents rooting for their tickets, nor do they threaten decapitation of their cabin mates with the weight of their overhead luggage and rattling bottles of booze.

Not for experienced travellers the plastic bags of duty free, the clank of bottles, the shame of cigarettes, some melting bars of chocolate and perfumed deodorants that could never conceal the malodorous results of hurrying and hoisting luggage since dawn. Experienced travellers do not tote soggy sandwiches and Styrofoam cups, nor squashed newspapers rolled up in the free copy of the in-flight magazine. They have a bottle of cool water for thirst, a book to read, the seat that does not squeak and a non-chalance that ignores the herd of heaving luggage luggers around them.

Light packers are spared the panic that the heavy packers endure: realising they have forgotten the basics despite all their baggage and that the last time they saw their credit cards was on the kitchen table as the taxi honked the horn.

Light packers have lists. They know their itinerary. They have checked the temperature, the rainfall, their schedules, cultural customs, language and modes of address and all the details of their destination. They have chargers and voltage adaptors, crease-resistant attire and comfortable shoes, laminated maps and the pocket-sized edition of the best sights to see. They remember tickets and passports, laptop and iPod, camera and phone and the code to dial home.

As we sojourn in Italy, spend months in Provence, pop over to Prague, vacation in Venice and stop off in Spain, acquiring the art of packing is important in terms of stress. For while anal retention may characterise travellers who carry no more than a clutch bag, ditherers who cannot leave home without wardrobes, nor return without added suitcases bulging with souvenirs, must have no joy from their journeys away.

Now that increased weight restrictions mean decreased luggage, the optional element has gone from packing skill. If travel is not to be torture, we all have to learn how to compact pack. And if it's an art you truly cannot master, then most mentors would suggest that you either add a sense of humour to your holdall, or pack it all in and holiday at home.

Decluttering:
Hoarders and
Discarders

People are divided into two distinct categories with regard to possessions. These are hoarders and discarders, each of whom expresses their psychological status through their relationship with possessions.

Hoarders snaffle, store and smother their homes with the significant and sentimental. Discarders dispose of everything. What hoarders regard as precious, discarders regard as life's detritus. By these behaviours it is suggested that hoarders cling to the past while discarders reject it.

Therefore, while hoarders and discarders embrace a philosophy of living, they are opposites in how they live, with distinct recognisable behavioural repertoires. Each inhabit homes that reveal their assignment as hoarders or discarders, collectors, investors, rejecters or ejectors of objects from the first glimpse of the possessions that surround them, or lack thereof.

Hoarders and discarders view each other suspiciously as entirely separate emotional species. This is because being a hoarder or a discarder is not just a matter of taste. It is a matter of far more complex psychological significance.

From this psychological perspective, why one hoards or why one discards is the issue. The answer establishes whether the pattern of hoarding or discarding objects is one of psychological adjustment or pathological difficulty. The extremity of the behaviour determines the severity of the diagnosis!

In the heart of each hoarder lies a person who knows that to desist from retaining every object of emotional, archival or potential monetary value would evoke great anxiety, withdrawal and distress. Hoarders squirrel away possessions to preserve the memorabilia of their lives.

Each object carries a story, happy or sad, evidence of life and love, insurance for the winter of old age against the loneliness of isolation. Albums and objects of remembrance are retained to counteract the barrenness of being forgotten. Utensils are stored for a time when there may be no money to buy the things one needs.

In the heart of each discarder lies a person who wonders if minimalism is miserly or an attempt to disguise and hide 'selfhood' by discarding all clues to personality, preference, possession, person or the past. Not for the minimalist the photos of family on the mantel, fridge cluttered with children's drawings, mementoes, mess and kitsch or the souvenir sangria bottles from the first trip to Spain.

From a clinical perspective, the three main 'types' of hoarders are logical, sentimental and guilty. The logical hoarder knows that time determines the value of objects; that today's tack is tomorrow's profit. Often these hoarders are creative, lateral thinkers who imagine myriad uses for an object so that to discard one is to reject the potential multiple purposes a single object may provide.

The sentimental hoarder needs to consider why tangible evidence of past life and love is required. It is proposed that this archival need may stem from childhood deprivation of the memorabilia and photographs people require as records of their existence before their own memory can do so.

Among sentimental hoarders may be those bereaved, adopted or fostered in infancy, for whom objects provide identity or whose history is denied by their absence. In the absence of inheritance, objects are significant. Yet with an ironic twist, the children of sentimental hoarders, overwhelmed by excessive documentation of their lives, reject the 'recording' process, the films and photos that deny their enjoyment of living in the service of evidence of how their lives were lived.

Meanwhile, the guilty hoarder is a product of the 'waste not want not' time, when no money was available to replace things broken and when need, not fashion, dictated what a person wore.

And whether we are hoarders or discarders may also depend on the messages of childhood, cultural messages about taste and waste or prior experiences of poverty or luxury, which may dictate whether objects are 'things' held in high regard or utensils to use and discard.

Discarders may be logical, anxious or angry. Logical discarders understand that a new possession in limited space requires removal of the old. It is as psychologically simple and straight-forward as that.

But the anxious or angry discarder should consider if fear of retention is fear of memory or of commitment. Ruthless elimi-nation of keepsakes, ejection of objects or constant redecoration of the home, may suggest discomfort with marking one's space, claiming oneself, one's personal style, or declaring an identity other than fashion-dictated, planned obsolescence wherein the self is erased by 'good taste'.

Whether a hoarder or discarder, there are questions of psychological import to be asked. What is my most precious possession? What are the other objects with which I surround or do not allow myself and why? What value do I place on them? Is this determined by the giver, the spirit in which they were given or by their monetary worth? What emotions are attached to the things I own? Which remind me of something, of someone or some time of significance in my life? If I could retain only three objects, what would I choose?

Whether hoarders or discarders, our possessions provide psychological insight into the self. Past and present, interests and activities are evident in the litter of our lives. The need to have confronts having no needs: the simplicity of enough challenges the burden of excess. The balance we keep on what we keep is one signifier of psychological health.

To shred all evidence of the past may be to deny that past. To keep all evidence of the past may be to deny the future.

What do you have at home?

LETTERS' LAST
POSTING

―――――――――

E-mail is a long way from snail mail. Far removed from the structure of the letter, written in one's 'best hand', each sentence measured, each paragraph providing additional considered information to inform, amuse, request, convey or simply keep in touch.

Once there was an art to letter writing: a different art from that of e-mail. Letters had formalities, niceties, required modes of address to recipients, structures, special salutations and conclusions, depending on your relationship with the recipient. Unlike e-mail, the written letter did not end abruptly: no CU2moro at the end of it with perhaps a smiley face or devilish grin thrown in for good measure.

Each communication was signed according to custom – yours faithfully, sincerely, affectionately, respectfully. Affability and humility vied in the signatory's concluding cordialities. Letters were populated with loving sons, devoted daughters, affectionate nieces and, indeed, obedient servants. These concluders have been replaced in texts today by such alphabetic brevity as BCNU (be seeing you), TTFN (ta ta for now) or TTYL (talk to you later), without an obedient servant in sight.

Letter writing was a formal business. Etiquette demanded ink, fine bonded stationery, heavier for formal communication, lighter or tissue-thin for foreign missives which could take days or weeks to arrive depending on their destination.

Good taste dictated discretely coloured paper – white, grey, granite and blue – being acceptable with matching envelopes shaped according to the type of correspondence involved. Lined paper was to be avoided at all costs, while pages from a copybook were the ultimate act of disregard, even for the most casual of communications.

But most important was the 'good hand', the stamp of education, testimony to one's neatness, order, exactitude and control of pen and person. Script was to be clear, uniform, disciplined and legible, descended from the calligraphic 'rustic capitals' and 'square capitals' and the 'Carolingian minuscule' – the derivatives of which generations of schoolchildren practised letter by letter in lined writing copies in order to perfect their penmanship so that it did not tail off across the page into minuscule diagonal illegibility.

The address on envelopes was not written in haste but commenced just a tad below the mid-point of the envelope, preferably to contain paper folded evenly once within the envelope so that upon extraction the letter opened right-side up, ready to be read. As for the addressees, what a wonderful term was Messrs: once the mode of address for brothers or business partners, it is now more likely to be a description of disruptive schoolboys.

Then there were the Misses, Miss, Master and Esquire. There was, of course, Mr and Mrs followed by the Christian and surname of the husband. Even Mrs when she was addressed alone was followed by her husband's names, subsuming her gender and identity under that of the male name. Meanwhile, whole hierarchies of other titles ranked, filed and compartmentalised people in what now seem to be the most odd and unequal ways.

But have all the changes in communication changed our actual communication? What is the difference, if any, between receiving a carefully composed communication written in the sender's best hand on elegant paper enfolded in an envelope or the e-mail popping up somewhat magically upon the screen? Is there greater anticipation when one recognises the writing upon an envelope as being from family or friends or when the name of the sender of the e-mail appears? Have changes in the mode and medium of communication altered the psychology of how we relate to each other? Or does new technology simply provide more immediate ways of saying the same kind of things we have always said?

Does it matter if the question is an abbreviated RUOK as opposed to 'my dearest daughter, I hope that this letter finds you happy and in good health'? Was the expression of emotions in past missives so formatted that it had a perfunctory solicitude? Or did we say more, care more, communicate more and consider more before instant text and e-mail, which leaves mere seconds between our thoughts and the communication of them.

We live our lives at the time that we live them and we express our emotions through the media available to us at that time. There is no less heartbreak after a 'Dear John' letter than after a text that ends a relationship in abbreviated alphabetic form. The message is the same: it spells rejection whether it is done with brevity or in written form. Life, love and loss hit us with the same magnitude, whether we express them in flowery phrases or on mobile phones.

The expression of anger, which the immediacy of e-mail does not restrain, may have been delayed and allowed to abate by the process of writing, stamping and posting. But if instant anger is facilitated, so too are the instant communications of care, regret and concern that e-mails allow and that often bring us closer to each other in a different way.

Children on the other side of the world can remain in reassuring, chatty dialogue with home. Parents know that their offspring have arrived safely at foreign destinations. As they backpack across the world visiting cultures that were once mere pictures in a geographical encyclopaedia, parents can now receive photographic evidence of their children's whereabouts and well-being.

Good news is instant and sad news gets to those who need to know at once. We are with each other, even as we are apart, a mere communiqué away. Groups can gather spontaneously, families congregate easily, concerns may be allayed instantaneously, and distress and danger signalled directly. No more is one stranded by a breakdown, lost looking for an address or forced in times of trauma to rush to broken public telephones when emergency help is required. There is no need for belated birthday greetings, nor need one be late in sending congratulations or condolences or prevented from telling someone that they care.

But what of posterity? Can it take care of itself? Or do we delete all records of our lives so that in the future there will be no ribbon-tied letters to witness relationships? Will there be no embossed chronology of the development of love, the passage of time, the growth of relationships, the mementoes for later life, evidence that one was once young and loved and lived and hoped and dreamed?

Will there be no more attics with treasure chests of memories, no more parchments to decipher that uncover unknown aspects of our ancestors' lives, no more memoirs, no journals recording life as lived?

Will the creative process go unrecorded so that the decisions writers make to revise their characters, to soften or strengthen their natures, to alter dialogue, to change their stories' endings, may be lost forever, deleted in favour of the final revised version, the updated document, with nothing of its germination left to inform those who would wish to follow writers' cognitive paths? Why was one word chosen above another, and then another word considered before another word retained? What made that sentence redundant in the writer's mind, that paragraph inserted, the page torn out?

How will we track the progress of our mental processes? How will we record the ordinary, the everyday, life as lived in a particular time? Will social history die? Will history be recorded? Will creativity be hidden? Will we digitally document all that we wish to keep, or will the process of thought in creative and extraordinary minds be lost forever?

With these questions, I sign off. I have the honour to remain, dear reader, your humble and obedient servant. C U L8R

BODY LANGUAGE

A nod is as good as a wink. Or is it? Can you distinguish a sneer from a leer? Do you know what you show by those gestures or many other signals you may inadvertently send?

Each day, in a thousand ways, we communicate: not with words, but in the non-verbal world of what is described as 'analogic' communication, kinesics, paralanguage, corporal communication or body language. And it conveys myriad messages about us. Each facial expression, eye dilation, lip elongation, brow raise, eye blink, wink, chin thrust, mouth purse, nose curl, teeth gnash or lip twitch sends a powerful communication to observers.

This is the information we express when we 'say nothing at all' and it is received, read, interpreted and acted upon, often without recipients being consciously aware of what has triggered their response. Equally, we may be unaware that we have provided such insights into our personal worlds.

We may imagine that as a species we have replaced primitive communication with language. That is not so. Linguists, sociologists, anthropologists, neurologists and psychologists affirm that our capacity to send and receive non-verbal messages remains a powerful and primary communicative means.

As distinguished anthropologist Gregory Bateson observed, paralanguage evolved alongside verbal language and an important evolutionary stage was reached when we realised that such signals can be 'trusted, distrusted, falsified, denied, amplified, corrected and so forth'. This is what makes the poker player inscrutable. Forensic psychology also includes analysis of intentionally deceptive signals. We shudder at the cold countenance of the psychopath, the premeditated murderer's impenetrability: the absence of signals of concern.

Women are reportedly more proficient than men at reading complex non-verbal cues. Children quickly, although often ineffectively, try to conceal telltale signals, giving themselves away in the process. Think of the 'hand over mouth' covering surreptitious eating or classroom chat, the careful movements of stealth upon which mothers asked 'what are you up to?'

Consider the over-attentive countenance when mischief was afoot, the wide-eyed innocence, crocodile tears, judged not by lacrimal leakage but by exaggerated facial expression, or the gaze-avoidant guilty look so recognisable to teachers, even if one tried to brazen it out with a cheeky stare. This confirmed for children the truth of elders' claims to have eyes in the back of their heads, or in the words of Dante, 'if you had a hundred masks upon your face, your thoughts however slight would not be hidden from me'.

The prevalence of kinesics is evident from the many terms woven into our vocabulary. Who could forget the range of childhood incidents precipitated by an inadvertent facial expression or body posture? How many children have been startled by an adult command to take that smirk off your face without knowing what precise facial expression warranted such a reaction?

Annoyance was also evoked by what were called sullen looks. Gaze avoidance causes universal discomfort but is also a defence in children when rebuked, thereby eliciting the command to look at the admonisher. Myopia or astigmatism were no mitigation in determinations of shifty or sly-eyed looks, while every schoolgoer knew that shoulder shrugging was guaranteed to anger.

Dangerous, too, amongst peers, was inadvertent 'gawking', provoking intimidating interrogation by local bullies as to whom one was looking at, or more accurately *'what are you gawking at?'* This required immediate eye-aversion, humble denial and swift departure elsewhere, unless one was foolish enough, or hardy enough, to engage in the inane 'I'm looking at you, kangaroo' retort that precipitated non-verbal engagement of an entirely different kind!

What is not often understood, however, is that fear of being disbelieved sends the same non-verbal signal as fear of being caught out. Who could forget the class interrogation of likely larcenists when items went 'missing' from school lockers? The line-up of potential culprits identified the innocent more often than the guilty; less angst being the attribute of less-developed consciences.

Adolescents often smile when they are anxious, conveying, incorrectly, amusement or disdain instead of stress. Adolescent embarrassment may be camouflaged by conspiratorial giggling, this attempt to 'save face' often inspiring unwarranted wrath.

Few would misinterpret the arrogance conveyed by hands on hips, the disdainful ennui of eye-rolling, the warning in a clenched fist, raised hand, narrowing eyes, the difference between a smile and gritted teeth or the 'cold shoulder' exclusion from the group. Charles Darwin's famous study *The Expression of the Emotions in Man and Animals* identified the universality of facial expressions of disgust, hate, sadness, shame, anguish and guilt.

Other signs are cultural: thumbs up, fingers crossed, 'V' sign versus two-fingered gestures; greeting signals such as the Japanese greeting bow; proximal 'tie-signs' such as holding hands or grooming behaviours identifying closeness.

Disappointment is often disguised by false signals of exaggerated delight; witness the Oscars, where nominees who do not win conceal disappointment by displaying more delight than winners. And the terms 'postural echo' and 'isopraxis' refer to our human mimicry of each other in manner and dress, audience response, team colours, fashions and fads to keep our plumage similar and connected to each other.

It is not just our eyes that act as windows to the soul. We are bound and bonded together by the universality of our experiences, our signs and signals, showing emotion, inviting courtship, conveying sympathy, enabling empathy: gestures of affection, appeasement and of peace. We are more similar than different, more together than apart.

SENSE OR SENSIBILITY
(SYNAESTHESIA)

Can you imagine seeing colours when you hear music: hearing the colours of Fauré's *Pavane* or Tchaikovsky's *Chanson Triste*? What coloured cascades might Mozart's music bring? What gathering lights or whites Debussy's *Clair de Lune*? And would Vivaldi evoke traditional seasonal 'tones' or would each note provide a different coloured shade of sound?

These are the kind of questions cognitive neuroscientists and neuropsychologists studying the intriguing condition known as synaesthesia might ask as part of their constant quest to understand how the brain determines mind.

The word 'synaesthesia' derives from the Greek word for union of the senses, with *syn* meaning shared and *aesthesis* meaning sensation. It relates to that most captivating condition where stimulating one sense triggers another, so that you may conceivably taste shape, smell colour and see sound. This is involuntary sensory cross-activation and those people, known as synaesthetes, who experience such hybrid vibrations may not know, for some time, that other people do not share their rich intersensorial world in the same way.

Researchers into synaesthesia particularly emphasise the involuntary nature of the experience compared to the deliberate use of metaphor, contrived creative interchange of co-sensory words in literature and poetry, literary tropes or sought sensory fusion in audiovisual, spatial or multisensory music. Nor is it the same as drug-induced pseudosynaesthesia, such as is caused by LSD, which 1960s psychedelic filmic versions of this experience presented to the generation of young people at that time.

The literature on synaesthesia is vast, highlighting that it runs in families with more women than men (ratios from 3:1 to 8:1 are quoted), that there is a tendency to be left-handed, to have an excellent memory, and there is debate about whether it is present in all infants and subsequently lost, whether more artistic, intuitive, psychic and creative people are synaesthetes and in what circumstances it may help or hinder a person

References to synaesthesia extend back to Isaac Newton's observations that there was a parallel between colours of the spectrum and the notes on a musical scale, from which he designed a colour music wheel. However, it is only in recent times that significant interdisciplinary attention has been paid to synaesthesia, as the technology of brain functional imaging (fMRI) allows us to observe the brain in action, record subjective experience and to revise ideas about the brain as self-contained subsystems. As US researcher Richard Cytowic writes, 'although medicine has known about synaesthesia for three centuries, it keeps forgetting that it knows'.

But this is a condition that it behoves us to remember because of the insight it may provide into the working of the brain: into memory, modes of learning and detailed recall. Many synaesthetes report amazing memory for poems, prose and dialogue and have superior photographic spatial recall, with a mental map of the exact location of a book on a shelf, a poem in a book or an object in the garden shed.

Understanding synaesthesia may provide more information on sensation and perception, the connections between reason and emotion and conscious and unconscious processes.

There is significant controversy as to whether understanding synaesthesia might provide more understanding of conditions such as dyslexia because many synaesthetes see letters or words in colour; whether it might provide insight into dyscalculia, or problems in mathematical reasoning; or give greater understanding of allochiria, which is right-left confusion, poor sense of direction and even experiences of déjà vu and psychic phenomenon.

Perhaps there are more ordinary experiences. Our language is replete with images that show our accessibility to this fusion of feelings engendered by the senses. We speak of loud colours and heavy tones, sharp sounds, vivid smells and the bitter word. And we speak of cheerful yellow and we often sing the blues and we *see* what we mean when we say these things. This is why some thinkers, such as the Russian scientist Bulat Galeyev, believe we may misunderstand synaesthesia, that each of us carries the potential to capture, sensitively and with sensuality, the world of beauty, the world of art and artistry, the *aesthetic* world, which, Galeyev reminds us, is another ancient Greek word from which synaesthesia may derive.

Certainly there are many artists and poets identified as synaesthetes who have translated their co-sensory experiences of imaginary endeavours for us. So what can we say about the musicality of colour and the chromatism of music? Well, think of the artist David Hockney. Just look at his painting *A Bigger Splash* for a vision of that sound, or Jackson Pollock's dripping, smearing paint, or artist František Kupka's *Discs of Newton* or *Piano*

Keyboard Lake, based on the colour music code of scientist Hermann von Helmholtz. Think of the works of Kandinsky, the music of Liszt translating the writings of Hugo, Byron and Goethe into music.

But why is our own James Joyce not on this list? In *Ulysses* does he not show membership of the world of synaesthetes with the words, 'he could hear, of course, all kinds of words changing colour, like those crabs about Ringsend in the morning burrowing quickly into all colours of different sorts'.

Synaesthesia captures our imagination. It is the place where science and art collide, where philosophy, neurology, genetics and psychology reside and coincide: for if we look at the brain, in what part does poetry lie, where in the occipital lobe is the artist?

We know that we are more, much more, than sensory and neuronal paths, however complex these may be, and that these physiological pathways are passages to imagination and corridors of creativity to possibilities beyond.

The Meaning
of Manners

The rules of etiquette have little to do with our world today. Regarded as the secret code of a bygone era, by design they distinguished between those who were 'well derived' and people of so-called social inconsequence. Aristocratic status provided almost automatic admittance to select circles. For others, their speech, manner, dress and deportment identified them as unworthy of invitation to genteel society.

In former times it was essential that a 'lady' conducted herself with propriety. Displays of emotion were unseemly. Modesty, manners, gentility, decorum and demureness were essential lady-like demeanours. Flaunting oneself was unbecoming. Suggestions of 'romantic interest' were strictly the prerogative of men. Women who indicated any such inclinations, such lack of refinement or 'forwardness' were consigned to the realm of 'wantonness'. Fine lines were also drawn between being coquettish, flirtatious and coy.

Life was laced with behavioural terminology affirming charm, affability, cordiality, delicacy and dignity. Alternatively, vanity, folly, insensibility and breeches of etiquette were decried and punished harshly. Gentlemen were equally obliged to observe complex behavioural codes, being careful to address only those ladies to whom they had been introduced and never taking the vacant seat next to a woman not of their acquaintance.

Ladies were not subjected to harsh, coarse or crude language and 'retired' after dinner to allow men to enjoy their cigars, to pass the port (of course to the right) and to engage in discussion not necessarily fit for delicate ears. Besides, there were philosophical positions, political affairs and the concerns of state to be deliberated upon (the intellect of women, of course, being unable for such matters).

Does not Jane Austen in *Northanger Abbey* make it abundantly clear that 'a woman, especially, if she has the misfortunate of knowing anything, should conceal it as well as she can'? Clearly, anything so gross as academic interest or evidence of intellect was not high on the list of feminine charms likely to engage male interest in times past. Of course, gentle readers, there are some so bold as to suggest that, in that particular, time has occasioned little change!

Yet over the years the rules of social interaction have changed significantly. What was *de rigeur* at one time would be ridiculed today. How many men and women commuting to and from their daily employment are in circumstances that require changes of attire between morning, afternoon and evening, unless it be the change for the gym or a swim before or after work? Being 'at home' is more likely to be due to sick leave from work.

As for dressing for dinner, the TV tray hardly requires black tie, the symmetry of silver settings or glasses for each beverage and John Betjeman might not require Norman to 'phone for the fishknives' any more. Few formalities surround the after-dinner cuppa, which is now more likely to be a mug, a vessel not necessitating an extended little finger whilst supping. Calling your 'napkin' a 'serviette' has ceased to be a punishable offence and 'an elegant sufficiency' is quite simply 'enough'.

Social interactions have changed exponentially. Informality has replaced earlier forms of address: first-name exchange being almost immediate, while the couple and chaperone of former days is now likely to be a threesome of a very different kind. Third person invitations and replies are confined to more formal events, dispensing with the need to reach for *Debrett's* daily for envelope etiquette when the 'send' e-mail icon can deliver immediately.

Pomposity has become a source of comedy, a parody on protocol exemplified by the suburban absurdity of TV character Hyacinth Bucket (pronounced Bouquet, of course) devoted to delusions of grandeur, of falsity and façade. Yet within her we find a resonance of the inner affectedness that we fear resides in our subconscious selves or that we have witnessed in some measure in the affectations of others, however much they have attempted to conceal them. We laugh because we fear that there lingers a dormant desire to soften the sharper aspects of life with these predictable, protective proprieties. We laugh because there is no place for posturing in our post-modern world.

There are many who welcome this passing of what they believe was pageantry and pretension, who reject the formalities of what they associate with an oppressive colonial past that has no cultural relevance to the Ireland of this era. Egalitarian society cannot continue to countenance privilege based on such discriminatory ways. There is no place for U and non-U and the linguistic distinctions that divided them.

But there are also people who distinguish between the inane aspects of earlier etiquette and the modern merits of good manners: polite practices, decency, civility, understatement and respect for others. They lament the passing of simple politeness, the common courtesies, the written thank you note on receipt of a gift, the bus seat vacated for older occupants, the door held open, the apology upon inadvertent offence, the offer of assistance when obviously required, and just some restraint in what is spoken about and how it is said. They are concerned that there has been an over-correction whereby the crude, rude and crass have become commonplace, as if politeness is politically incorrect.

For manners maketh the psychological milieu in which we live, they say, and perhaps they are right.

So, gentle reader, lest I appear too bold in my persuasions, too dogmatic of disposition, imprudent in opinion, too unyielding and decisive in character and indecorous in the manner of my writing; rather than my doing so, I beg *you* to determine the merits of manners in our world.

EMOTIONS
AND
BEHAVIOURS

Introduction

The human emotional and behavioural repertoire is staggering in its variety and vocabulary. An alphabetic range of emotions and behaviours awaits our enactment: affection, antagonism, anger, benevolence, betrayal, cruelty, caution, care, delight, desire, empathy, enthusiasm, earnestness, fear, failure, gratitude, garrulousness, hope and heroism, insight, intuition and invention, jealousy and kindness and kinship, love, lechery and laughter, melancholy and mourning, narcissism and optimism, pride, poise, paranoia and perfection, querulousness and quiescence, revulsion, restlessness and revenge, sacrifice, secretiveness, sagacity and temerity, tenaciousness and tenderness, uncertainty, unreasonableness and uxoriousness, vanity, viciousness and vacillation, wishing, waiting, wailing and weeping, xenophobia, yelling and yawning, zealousness and zoophobia to name but a few!

But it is not just the emotions that we feel but also the emotional vocabulary that we acquire with which to articulate feelings that is central to how we interpret ourselves, and others, as we react to everyday, ordinary and extraordinary life. Emotions and behaviours are inextricably linked and if one has control over the former, the latter usually concur and are under control. A dictionary of emotions is, therefore, not as bizarre as it may first appear in the list above, for to know is to name, to name is to validate, to verify is to authenticate the veracity of the experience and the vocabulary of life.

The essays in this section explore a number of primary emotions and behaviours. From the trivial to the tragic, along the emotional continuum of living, lie the agony and ecstasy of life, without whose polarities the richness of living would be dampened down and neither domain would have the magnitude they encompass by virtue of the other. And so we consider happiness, elusive as we pursue it, seeking it where it is not to be found, finding it when we cease the search, recognising it when it is naked, mistaking it when it is clothed in bright garments that glimmer deceptively.

Vanity and its remedies remains a cosmetic challenge of our time. 'Against the assault of laughter nothing can stand,' said Mark Twain. So too is a smile disarming and therefore miles of smiles must have ecosystemic impact engendering happiness and enjoining us to count our blessings in gratitude for the pleasantries of life. We are more than living creatures; we are hemathermal, sentient, perceptive, expressive beings. We feel. We conceal our vanities. We retch at injustice. We encounter regret and remorse when our behaviour is asynchronous with our inner belief about how we should be. We are capable of cruelty of unimaginable kind, particularly when, as Polish writer Czeslaw Milosz argued in his letter to Jerzy Andrzejewski, 'rationalisations come to the aid of sadism'. Yet juxtaposed with our cruelty is our equal and astonishing heroism, the redemption of sacrifice, our capacity for hope and the salvation of that supreme, superlative incomparable human emotion, love.

SMILING

Smiling is a human signal. It serves a primitive survival function. It is a key element in bonding. It is one of the strongest
infant signals, the glue that entices and enthrals new parents,
keeping them close and rewarding them for their presence. For
who can leave a baby's beguiling smile to attend to anything else?

Crying may summon parents to their baby's side, but the
smile retains them. Once smiled at, parents are smitten.

Smiling encourages care taking. It helps children to engage
with other children. It is disarming in adolescents, reassuring
between adults and well established in older people whose smile
lines map their lives. This is why radical cosmetic surgery is so dis-
concerting: it contorts human expression, sending contradictory
signals to observers.

While smiling is usually associated with positive intent, not all
smiles are positive social signals. The communicative complexity
of the smile means that interpreting the nuances, the distinctions
between smiles, is a crucial skill. For there may be little lip varia-
tion between the grimace, the greeting and the grin, but aeons of
primitive psychological information separate them.

Smiling is the advance signal of the person who is approaching, usually indicating that the anticipated encounter will be

cordial, convivial and sociable. It is the equivalent of saying 'I come in peace'. This is one of the most common functions of the smile.

The smile is also a signal of recognition as one approaches a friend. Before speech can be heard, the smile can be seen, so that it prepares both parties for the encounter. One of the easiest detectable body language signs of tension between people is therefore the aversion of gaze and absence of a smile between people who know each other. Conversely, couples that are irritated with each other in a public space may conduct their whispered arguments with fixed smiles that are a social attempt to conceal the nature of their exchange. But the smiles face outwards and not towards each other. In this way the action of smiling, the nature of the smile, its direction and its duration all send important messages about relationships.

Smiles may be formal, friendly, flattering or flagrantly flirtatious. Smiling may be haughty and autocratic, as if a favour has been bestowed. The polite smile often conveys unspoken disapproval. Smiles may be dismissive or malicious, simpering or superior, shy, supercilious or conciliatory. There are sly, snide, sneering, sarcastic and spiteful smiles. There are smiles that are contemptuous, casual or cruel. There are smiles that are warm, affirming and supportive: that gather us into the group.

When we receive a smile, we respond emotionally to what we see. Psychological distress occurs when there is a discrepancy between a person's facial expression and tone of voice. Dissonance confuses us. The difference between teeth displayed in humour and teeth gritted in anger, while almost immeasurable physically, is enormous in emotional terms.

Smiles may be conspiratorial when exchanged between two people in communicative collusion against a third. They are powerful weaponry in the non-verbal arsenal of bullying. People can denigrate with the downturn of a lip.

Smiles are the stuff of film close-ups: the visual information that identifies the villain's smile of subterfuge and deceit. This powerful filmic mechanism of contradictory signals is what makes such images chilling. When the scoundrel smiles, all is lost. Film director Alfred Hitchcock resourced this incongruity between humour and cruelty, using it to powerful effect.

Children are acute observers of smiles: they notice dissonance between signals. They check, not just the smiling person's mouth, but also their eyes. For eyes and mouth together determine the veracity of a smile.

The coy smile sends another contradictory message, being both bashful and invitational simultaneously. The wry smile betrays cynicism, a sardonic signal that may be scathing in its brevity. The placatory smile has a protective and defensive role where appeasement is required.

The amused smile signals inner laughter whereas the bemused smile indicates inner bafflement, uncertainty about the validity, reality or normality of what one is seeing and a level of disbelief in it. Beloved of candid camera footage are these perplexed, bemused and secret smiles of people confronted with odd or aberrant behaviour. When we watch such footage, we in turn smile empathically, knowing that our response would be similar if we were in that situation.

The brave smile signals determination to overcome all obstacles. The smile of resignation shows that the contest is over. The grateful smile is all the appreciation most people ever need. The gentle smile is healing.

Smiling has a role, a function and a purpose in human interaction. From a psychological perspective, the impact of encountering people who greet with a smile rather than a frown, with humour rather than discontent and with affability rather than anger is far more significant than is consciously realised. The facial expressions, even of unknown passers-by, can invade our day. We live, not as isolated creatures, but as part of communities whose general temperament and temper influence our own humour and sense of well-being.

Which is why the children's smiling rhyme may be a useful mental health prescription: that is to 'smile a while and while you smile another smiles and soon there's miles and miles of smiles and life's worthwhile because you smile'.

HAPPINESS

Happiness is elusive. It is the state that is most desired, least defined and most difficult to attain. Even when acquired it is not always recognised, so that it becomes apparent by its absence when it is lost. It is then that we wish that we had savoured what we had and wish we had known how lucky we were.

Happiness cannot be bought. It is least obtainable when it is actively sought. It is achieved through neither hedonism nor asceticism, particularly when gaining happiness is the goal. Happiness cannot be sold, but the belief that it can be produced, packaged and purchased is big business. It brings wealth to those who peddle promises of pleasure and it brings disappointment to those who believe that happiness can be got in this way.

Wealth does not guarantee happiness. While it may be better to be miserable in comfort than in poverty, and while there is an inevitable link between poverty and unhappiness, having wealth does not automatically mean feeling good. Research into the happiness of lottery winners, for example, shows how little having possessions contributes to contentment and how often sudden acquisition of large sums of money can bring misery to those unprepared for the altered emotional dynamics with family, friends and society that can follow.

Additionally, while most people agree with the maxim 'health is wealth', it is usually not until one's health is threatened that we appreciate health as the ultimate wealth. Perspective on life is altered radically by the loss of health so that we truly experience the grief, identified by Dante, of recalling 'a time of happiness when in misery'.

Positive psychology supports the philosophical-theological perspective that longing for things makes us unhappy. Psychology has also attempted to identify the states, the traits, the types of people, the familial conditions, the educational experiences and the social environment most conducive to feelings of well-being, of self-esteem, of optimism and of happiness. There are no guarantees from any psychotherapy model that unmitigated happiness will be the outcome; rather, to paraphrase Sigmund Freud, the endeavour is simply to turn people's utter misery into 'normal human unhappiness'.

And this is important, for one of the major blocks to happiness that arises clinically is the belief that young people in particular have that they are somehow psychologically deficient if they are not happy all the time and that they are personally to blame if they seek a deeper meaning than self-indulgence in their lives. This is why existentialism may reassure them that it is all right to sometimes view our world as utterly absurd and to seek to redefine ourselves within it, to sometimes march to a different tune and to wish to compose one's own melody in life.

The requirement to be happy has been foisted upon us as a right, an obligation and a measure of our psychological stability, as if feelings of unhappiness are indices of psychological volatility and vulnerability. This makes the 'unhappy' feel guilty and the 'happy' feel anxious lest their current happiness be squandered or taken away. Instead, our major psychological challenge today might be to understand and tolerate the vicissitudes of life. It might be to accept that we are lucky if happiness visits sometimes, if tragedy does not strike, if we experience no more than the usual uncertainties, disappointments, losses, self-doubts and injustices that are the weave of living and of this life and if we can retain reasonable optimism when things go wrong.

The quest to discover, delineate, describe and define happiness is endless. For what is this happiness we seek? For some it is acceptance of oneself in all one's eccentricity. It is work well done. It is adversity overcome. It is something to do, someone to love and something to hope for. It is filling the hour. It is looking forward to tomorrow. It is getting through today. It is knowing that life will be better. It is being glad that things are good.

Happiness may be matching our wants to our possessions and our ambitions to our capacities. Alternatively, it may be Michelangelo's desiring 'more than we can accomplish', poet Robert Browning's joy in 'reaching beyond our grasp' or writer Nathaniel Hawthorne's acceptance that happiness, like 'the butterfly we chase, is likely to alight upon us when we sit'. For some people happiness is music that invades the soul. It is silence. It is solitude. It is holding a new novel or the tattered, much-thumbed copy of the text that we love best. It is a whole day gardening. It is sea and sky. It is fishing. It is walking. It is talking. It is righting a wrong. It is unexpected affirmation. It is being accepted by the crowd.

Happiness is loving and being loved. Happiness is people. It is friends. It is in the eyes of those we care about. It is letters received. It is cards that wish us luck. It is exams that go okay. It is a feeling, an emotion, a belief, an idea. It is holding one's newborn or one's own child's child. It is remembering former happiness and being glad of those memories that nothing can erase.

It is believing in future happiness. It is Horace's valuing the day and 'calling the day one's own'. It is not being emotionally anaesthetised. It is not asking if we are happy, for then it flies away.

But what is most extraordinary and significant in all the work in relation to human happiness is that the ingredients that emerge most often as being useful in our quest for happiness are optimism, altruism, gratitude, forgiveness and fulfilment. This is because happiness is a form of love. Because love is a condition in which the happiness of another is essential to our own and research on happiness equally shows that our happiness increases when we give happiness away.

REGRET

Regret is a powerful human emotion. It usually occurs some time after the event to which it relates. It may be enhancing or self-defeating, immobilising or energising. In its deepest and most severe form, regret can lead to mental ill health.

Regret in its pure state may be reinforced by pain, anger, guilt or shame. Preoccupation with the past may obstruct the present and impede the future. Regret allied to guilt is usually toxic. Allied to forgiveness, including forgiveness of oneself, regret may provide healing of a special kind

Of course, regret may be instantaneous, as when a person realises that he or she has hurt or offended another person by irretrievable words. The problem with words is that one may regret but cannot retract them: the said cannot be unsaid.

More usually, however, regret arises from a more reflective perspective, whereby a person looks back at past events remorsefully. This often involves realisation of the significance of an opportunity lost that cannot be regained. It is more than insight. It is insight laden with sadness or guilt that what was done 'cannot be undone' or that what was not done is no longer possible.

It is the irretrievability of opportunity that deepens regret. Sometimes there is just one moment in which to say the right thing, to do the noble deed, ask the significant question, give the appropriate sympathy, make the visit, help the person who feels defeated or celebrate with friends who have achieved their life dreams.

There is a moment to say 'well done' or 'hard luck', to attend a funeral, write a letter, make a phone call, send the e-mail or text and let another person know that what is happening in that person's life is also important to you. Equally, there is often one moment to stand up for oneself, to assert individuality, resist coercion, declare beliefs, defend one's ideas and demand respectful treatment.

This is why regret is time-related. It is often expressed as a wish that one could turn back time, take a different and wiser path, follow a 'road less travelled', choose another route, alter a response, change a relationship, amend past incidents or even alter the entire course of one's personal life.

Psychological literature suggests that regrets occur primarily with regard to education, career, intimacy and parenting. But in the clinical context, what frequently arises are regrets about what was not said to someone, words that now cannot be said because that person has died. Grandchildren often wish they had told their grandparents how important a role they played in their childhood lives. Nieces and nephews regret that not until adulthood did they appreciate the contribution of their aunts or uncles to their emotional well-being.

Deathbed moments pass without the words that people wished to say being spoken and untimely death can rob those who are left of any chance to do or say what they would have said if they had known that tragedy would strike. There is often regret about what might have been said to parents before they died, regret about the questions not asked, the stories not clarified, the details of the family history not documented, the past that dies with a parent that has not been passed on because it was not asked about in time or because it never seemed to be the right time to ask.

Sons are sorry that they could not tell their father that they loved them or that they had to hear from other people that they had made their father proud. Daughters may wait a lifetime to receive maternal recognition and many parents never get told that the job they did was good. Valued friends may not hear how significant they were. Love is often carried to the grave.

While insightful regret may be useful, prolonged regret is counterproductive. The idea that future events are crucially conditional upon past choices is sometimes too firmly held. These 'if only' antecedent propositions can be powerful in shaping what we believe are consequent events. Carried to extremes, we can enter into the world of so-called counterfactuals: of possible or impossible worlds that could have been, would have been or might have been if things had happened differently.

This lends too much power to the past. After all, the road we did not travel might have been bumpier than the one we chose. We cannot tell. Maybe the richness of life would have bypassed us if we had taken more predictable paths. Maybe what we did and said and what was said to us was enough, and if we wish that it was more or less, that may be because we have insight now rather than that errors were made at that time.

For we need to remember that the unsaid is usually known, that when we regret what we did not do in the past it is from the perspective of the present that we make that analysis. We probably did what we could at the time and we should not judge ourselves by what would be possible for us to do today. When we are young we do not have the benefit of time, the experience of parenting and the perspective of the present to inform us. Hindsight can be harsh. Retrospect can be ruthless. Guilt is destructive.

What makes the words of Frank Sinatra's 'I did it my way' so powerful is that they universalise the reality of regret and rationalise the right to live our lives our own way. They reassure us that having a few regrets is human, that life can deal highs and lows, triumphs and blows as we live our lives our own way.

As to regrets about the unsaid in this article: sometimes we have to let things go, to accept that what is possible is not perfect, that often there are no perfect words, but the words that arrive as we write, that to write is to say something and there are always others who can add more. No regrets.

GRATITUDE

'Life remains a blessing,
Although you cannot bless.'

W.H. Auden

'Count your blessings' must be one of the least comforting and most irritating clichés. To anyone in the throes of loss, whether that be the loss of health, wealth or relationships, the advice to do so is always unwelcome. Its subtext says that regardless of the affliction that has befallen you, you ought to be appreciative of what you have. It suggests that you should feel guilty for grumbling when your 'lot' is much less unhappy than that with which others have had to contend. It admonishes you to gauge the gifts, not engage with the losses in your life.

This is a 'repellent strategy' according to Carol Shields' character in the novel *Unless*, as if 'dramatic loss can be replaced by the renewed appreciation of all one has been given'. Not only that, but failure to count blessings hints at gross ingratitude for the gifts which have been granted in one's life. It implies unworthiness to have received all that you have, when you are so churlish as to grieve for what you do not have. It is the ultimate guilt trip inflicted on the already distressed. It plunges those who are depressed deeper into self-deprecation. It exacerbates what it attempts to alleviate.

In summary, 'count your blessings' is the most miserable, maladroit, malodorous, odious expression against which there ought to be some law on grounds of incitement to self-hate. Because we cannot but feel bad about ourselves if someone thinks we have nothing to feel bad about.

When there is a trivial setback in one's life, being advised to count one's blessings may be experienced as an innocuous irritant enunciated by the less socially adroit. One can forgive it and ironically count amongst one's personal blessings the insight never to say something so clichéd to anyone else.

But there are times when suggesting that someone count their blessings is not just a *faux pas*. Times when it is a comment of such stupefying crudity that it borders on cruelty, as in one circumstance in which parents who lost a child were reminded to count the blessing of the other children they had. What a thing to say! This, alongside other chestnuts of comfort, is not comforting. Silence and sympathetic presence are what we need most when we are most needy and emotionally depleted.

Amongst the many victims of the enjoiner to count your blessings are mothers suffering from postnatal depression, who are reminded of the blessing of their beautiful baby, as if failure to do so is failure as a mother. Bad enough not to be able to live up to the images of idealised motherhood depicted on 'new baby' cards, but not to count oneself blessed by new motherhood is an indictment indeed, one that too often prevents depressed mothers from seeking help.

It does not help the young man who feels that his life has no meaning, the past unhappy and the future hopeless, to be told that this is the time to appreciate the blessings he has. Such admonitions deepen despair.

There are no immediate mental remedies for a man or a woman when a long-term relationship ends. This is a major disappointment, an experience of rejection, an attack on self-esteem, adaptation to life without that companion and alteration of future plans. It is hard to count blessings when one is counting losses.

There is no space for creative enumeration of 'blessings' at the moment an exam is failed, a job not attained, when someone is ill, a spouse dies, a child is sick, a young person injured or an adult receives a terminal diagnosis. Absorbing bad news is an emotional process that needs time to adjust to what one has lost before being able to appreciate again some of the good things one has.

In psychological terms, blessings and afflictions are unrelated. When tragedy strikes, one does not counteract the other in some mathematical way.

Creativity knows no bounds when it comes to inflicting the term 'count your blessings'. It suggests to children who will not eat their dinner a connection between world starvation and clearing their carrots and peas. It says that at least the crashed car is insured, that the house that is flooded is adequately covered and for the missed flight you were lucky you could book another. It's a reminder that your lost possessions will benefit the finder. It tells those who have lost their wealth to be grateful for their health.

Therein lies the problem. There are times when it is advantageous to remember how lucky we are. There are times when we might actually benefit by reminding ourselves that, indeed, if we have our health that is sufficient wealth; that we eat when others starve; that we buy goods when others are dispossessed; that the unfortunate burglary at the foreign family holiday home is not the 'misfortune' of the homeless.

But we also need to recognise that there are no immunities to human suffering, that there are times when no quantifying of blessings will disqualify acute pain, that suffering occurs in a vacuum, a vortex from which people emerge in their own way, with time, understanding and loving support.

Our role, if any, is not to advise others to count their blessings, but to be a blessing that others can count on. That is what counts.

HOPE

People are heroic. The human capacity to cope with calamity, overcome adversity, adapt to hardship and surmount suffering is remarkable. And it is most remarkable when it takes the form of quiet fortitude: when a heroic life is lived day by day.

For the heroic act, however extraordinary, admirable and courageous it may be, is usually a singular identifiable deed well done, whereas the laudable life is one of sequential sacrifices that require renewed bravery each new day. This is not to denigrate the former in favour of the latter. But visible heroes are usually recognised, honoured and rewarded for their bravery, while everyday heroes rarely feature in the annals of awards.

Heroism is something that many people demonstrate every day. Often it is unobserved. Frequently it is unacknowledged. Sadly, many do not realise that their daily lives are odysseys that rival the most heroic Homeric tales, feats of the Fir Bolg and victories of the Tuatha De Danann. For they live valiant lives that challenge our most extravagant concepts of courage.

Most people know someone in this 'ordinary hero' league: people who live positively and optimistically, despite the outrageous misfortunes that have befallen them. Who does not know at least one person who has been weighted with excess illness or loaded with bewildering bad luck, afflicted with inexplicable adversity and allocated unfair portions of human hardship? And who could not admire the courage these ordinary people have?

Amongst these heroes are people who cope with chronic illness, who fight poor prognoses, who circumvent disablement, who confront addiction, who harness anxiety, who recognise their depression, who defy disfigurement, who manage awful illness and who endure what the rest of us would find unbearable. What about carers, those people who care for family members that are unable to look after themselves? Carers uncared for by society, health services, government assistance or legislative protection, heroes who engage, not in one heroic act, but in one heroic life in the service of others.

Many courageous people never give up on life. Hopelessness is not in their vocabulary. They carry the child who might be disabled, they cherish the life that is not perfect, they love and seek help for the disturbed adolescent who endlessly, mindlessly exhausts them each day. They protect the young adult who has a mental illness, they challenge the husband or wife who has alcoholism, they mind the parent whose mind has long since left their body until the body is ready to leave this life.

For some heroes, suffering is medical. Always it is loss. For to lose one's sight or hearing, capacity to walk, ability to talk, use of a limb, a skill, all reduce the armoury required to battle one's way through life. Yet heroes fight on when most others would have thrown down their arms or thrown up their arms in surrender.

Sometimes suffering means witnessing another person's angst. Helplessness when faced with the suffering of someone we love is suffering that often surpasses personal pain. For to endure one's own pain may be difficult, but to be unable to alleviate that of one's child, or spouse, or parent is a particular form of suffering that derives from deep empathy and profound love.

Sometimes suffering is without recognisable external cause, identifiable justification that one can articulate or that other people can understand. Depression's dark night of the soul is further overshadowed by guilt and self-revulsion at feeling depleted when ostensibly gifted with plenty. The courage of people who suffer from depression is heroic, because unlike the bruised limb and bandaged head, how does a person explain the sheer physicality of a suffering that is physically invisible?

Physical ailments are not confined to the body. Disability is not specific incapacity, it changes everything. It means that each day more energy is required to do what others do automatically. It means living a different life. Yet everyday heroes never give up. The next diagnosis is the next dispute with fate. The next disaster is the next opportunity to oppose oceanic troubles 'and by opposing end them'. For these audacious archers, 'the slings and arrows' of unfair fortune are caught and slung away.

Can psychology capture the essence of the ineffable heroism of everyday heroes? Can it capture the essence of hope? An extensive literature on the psychological benefits of hope exists, of which the studies on 'positive psychology', 'learned optimism' and 'authentic happiness' by psychologists such as Dr Martin Seligman are just one example.

Hope is one of psychology's resilience tools. It emerges at the edges of despair. It is coiled, ready to 'spring eternal in the human breast'. Hope encourages, for 'if winter comes, can spring be far behind?' Hope defies despair. It overcomes fear. It 'flies with swallow's wings'. It imagines reaching the most distant goal and by believing, gets there.

Hope is what keeps people alive when the prognosis says they should be dead. It may be the last, but it is the most important ingredient in survival. It is what emerges when Pandora's box is shut, releasing new resolve when all else seems to fail. It is 'the thing that perches in the soul and sings the tune without the words'.

It is the belief with which 'ordinary heroes' demonstrate not mere moments of bravery, but lifetimes of magnificent courage that give the rest of us reasons to hope.

CRUELTY

Research by Professor Samuel Gosling of the University of Texas suggests what animal lovers have always known, that animals indeed have their own characteristics, capacities and idiosyncrasies by which they may be distinguished. They are unique, formed in the relationship with humans who care for them.

This animal individuality, the inimitability of each animal, makes the question of 'breed' an ambivalent one. While there are distinctive lineage characteristics associated with specific breeds – to guard, protect, rescue and assist humans, traits which animal owners may occasionally boast of – owners equally do not usually wish to confine the attributes of their personal pets to the mere outcome of ancestry. Indeed, in instances where a breed has any negative ascriptions, owners will hasten to defend their personal pet from uniform descriptions.

Such is the love and relationship between man and his best friend that owner-to-owner conversations often include the latest accomplishment of their capable canines, while cat owners know the precision with which their cats chose them. No one who has read Alistair MacLeod's spectacularly beautiful novel, *No Great Mischief*, could have remained unmoved by the manner in which generations of MacDonald 'dogs', dogs that 'cared too

much' and 'tried too hard', intersect the transgenerational psychological history of the MacDonald clan.

The family pet is personal. In and through its relationship
with family members, it develops its own routines, anticipations,
reactions and behaviours and an understanding of selected human
expression and words. This comprehension is not confined to 'sit',
'fetch' and 'stay'. Dog owners who have found themselves spelling
the proposal of a 'W-A-L-K' to each other will know the degree
to which pets appropriate and incorporate the language of
routine; that their understanding of human ways and emotions is
stunning, as is their response, unerringly provided to humans in
need.

But there is a bigger issue than pet 'ownership'. It is the issue
of respect for all living things; the deeper dimensions of nature,
natural wisdom, existence and uniqueness. This is an issue about
which we must begin debate, and not cease until we have incor-
porated regard for all living creatures into our everyday lives and
laws. Not in some maudlin manner, but in practical understanding of nature, the seasonality of life and the powerful presence of
living creatures.

There are some who do this. Most livestock farmers understand the respectful reciprocity between animal and man, their
co-dependence and the mutuality of their existence. They
understand the land, nature's balance, nature's terms and the
importance of animals in the ecology of life.

But many people do not regard the life of animals of any
psychological consequence to them. And if, as Gosling's research
suggests and any human who has ever respected animals
will know, the individuality of the personality of animals is
observable and verifiable, then what onus lies on us as humans to
understand the capacity of that living being to suffer? How does

that colour our attitude to the fox fleeing for his life, the cat left dead, the dog abandoned, the sheep worried, the donkey over-burdened, the birds' habitats destroyed and the right of those who strike, kill or maim a living thing on the roadway to leave it in the dark coldness of its suffering to be hit again by the next car?

Physicists know that understanding begins with the tiniest particles. It was in the nucleus of the atom that power lay. Psychologists know that cruelty begins with the tiniest creatures. What we do to the 'least of creatures' we can do to all and our capacity for viciousness knows no bounds.

The casual, chilling cruelty inflicted upon animals is an issue of far greater psychological import than we are prepared to concede: the price more pernicious than we wish to admit. In the words of William Blake, 'each outcry of the hunted hare, a fibre from the brain does tear'.

Cruelty to animals in any form diminishes us emotionally, hardens us psychologically and delimits our definitions of suffering, of sensitivity and of human responsibility. It thus provides the crevice of carelessness towards living things that allows living carelessly in our environment. It is the first step in insensibility, the corridor to cruelty and the kernel of disregard for life forms, including our own.

For if we allow suffering in anything, we may allow suffering in everything.

SACRIFICE

———

Life is punctuated by events. There is a predictable Irish annual rhythm to existence. We celebrate Christmas, New Year, St Patrick's Day, Easter and Halloween, not to mention the many new multicultural religious rites and transnational traditions that we now embrace.

The seasons sequence the year. There are also national holidays, state occasions, sports fixtures, theatre festivals, musical celebrations. We enjoy science expositions, art exhibitions, literary revelries and historical anniversaries of national pride and shame.

In a curious way, these seasonal celebrations and cultural events delineate our days and they are psychologically significant regardless of the degree to which we participate or exempt ourselves from involvement in them. Perhaps this is because each occasion has its own images, collective interpretation, personal meaning and psychological import. Easter is no exception.

Our relationship with Easter is complex in Ireland because of the conjoining of Christian commemoration and political events such as the Easter Rising and the Good Friday Agreement. Additionally there is the commercial Easter: the celebration of new life as represented by the egg, now transformed, for children at least, into a concentrated, consumer chocolate fest.

Easter's religious images are psychologically potent. Dominant are those of suffering and sacrifice. Within Christian tradition there is a kind of annual angst in the routine of remembrance throughout Easter week. Easter is suffused with suffering, with the contradictions between cruelty and contrition, treachery and triumph, doubt and belief and death and resurrection. Suffering precedes salvation. Sacrifice brings redemption.

But what place do messages of self-sacrifice have in the world today and what does the science of psychology have to say about sacrificing the self in the service of others?

Psychological discourses that focus on the individual as primary, self-sufficient, independent and unfettered by the dependence of other people reject self-sacrifice as psychologically unhealthy. They relegate self-sacrifice to the category of self-defeating personality disorder. In this way of thinking, to help others excessively is to be helplessly dependent upon their affirmation or the respect of those who witness one's helpfulness.

From this perspective, self-sacrifice is perceived to be pathological and it is suggested that it be replaced by more self-serving, individual, utilitarian ideals. The implications of this individuality rather than family- and community-oriented altruistic behaviour are of concern as social capital is depleted and the role of carer is denigrated.

Sigmund Freud saw sexual urges and instincts as the driving force in human activity rather than altruism or self-sacrifice. Scientist Richard Dawkins, in *The Selfish Gene*, describes both selfishness and altruism as biologically determined. Although, as he says, they touch 'every aspect of our social lives, our fighting and cooperating, our greed and our generosity', self-sacrifice serves personal genetic continuity rather than philanthropy.

But there are theoretical perspectives which reject such

pragmatism and embrace the philosophical. Austrian psychiatrist Viktor Frankl asserts the importance of giving as the means by which the 'true' self is found. His approach, known as 'logotherapy', maintains that man's deepest desire is to search for meaning and purpose in life. Based on his own experiences as a survivor of the concentration camps, he proposes that from the experience of suffering, meaning may emerge.

Suffering, in his terms, while not sought, provides the sufferer with the unique opportunity to encounter himself or herself, to find personal strength of which they were previously unaware, to discover unknown personal resources and to gain insights only available to those who have endured those particular experiences.

It is not unusual for people who have, for example, gone through the dark night of the soul to emerge with an indefinable strength, which they harness in the service of others who are depressed. Survivors of suffering set up many voluntary organisations and bring their insights and support to others beginning that journey.

Professionals in any psychological domain have long been aware that the qualification they do not have and the gift they cannot give is the deep understanding of someone who has experienced what their client has suffered. It is not possible to imagine the experience of the death of one's child, the vigil with a dying parent, the terror of rape, the decline in physical or mental capacity, the torture of trauma, the loss of a spouse, the loneliness of abandonment, the isolation of separation, the burden of being a carer for years and years or the role of parenting a child with special needs and the fears for the future of that child. Who but those who have experienced it can speak about the suicide of a family member, the disablement of domestic violence, the treachery of betrayal, the despair of injustice, the indignity of dependency, the wretchedness of rejection and the despondency of grief?

And consider the generosity with which staggering numbers of people who arise from such personal suffering dedicate that experience to others. Consider the psychological complexities through which many believe that beneath their suffering lay an extraordinary if unwished for privilege, and an encounter with indefinable aspects of humanity at its most magnificent during its time of greatest vulnerability.

Easter is, perhaps, a celebration of those who 'watch one hour' with others and who give generously of themselves for other souls.

LOVE

———

L ove is essential to human survival. Survival depends on this
love. This human 'attachment' is usually defined as the mutually affectionate, emotional relationship and desire to maintain
closeness between two people. Often the first attachment is to the
mother. This is the first prototype of love. It is the model we inter-
nalise and bring to our adult relationships unless there is rupture,
disruption, deprivation or privation.

Studies of the human infant show that once attached, there is
distress at separation, pleasure at reunion and a constant aware-
ness of the caregiver. Life revolves around this loving presence. In
that presence there is security, arms that enfold and a shield
against the world. Without this love there may be physical and
emotional 'failure to thrive'. Indeed, to love and be loved is so
crucial to our development that a vast literature of psychological
research examines the consequences of the loss of the loved one on
a person's later capacity to love.

The famous, still relevant research by René Spitz in the 1940s
showed that the tiniest amongst us may become depressed if
deprived of love. His work described what he called 'anaclitic'
depression in orphaned institutionalised infants: infants who were
only provided with unloving perfunctory physical care by a series

of non-involved caretakers. And the later writings of psycho-analyst John Bowlby depict the painful phases an infant goes through when the love object is removed. This is a terrible sequence of protest, inconsolable crying and the soul-wrenching state of sadness before final desolation and resignation set in and the infant folds inwards upon itself.

Adult love and loss is not so different. We have celebrated it and elevated it in our search to understand it. It is the quest for the unattainable. The emotions of star-crossed lovers fill our minds and imaginations, our poetry, drama, opera and art in creative attempts to capture the incomprehensibility of the complexity of love. Impossibility creates passion. Love at its most romantic is unrequited, unconsummated or denied. Who cannot cry at *Madam Butterfly*, *Casablanca's* drama of departure or when Rhett Butler finally and frankly does not give a damn? The power of *Titanic* is in the passion before the cold sea envelops one lover, leaving the other to remember forever.

Romantic love is often depicted as ill fated or illicit. From the first forbidden fruit it is a dangerous business. Most of its metaphors are painful. It is something we fall into, fall out of, drown in or are pursued or imprisoned by. Our hearts are captured, and trapped. Love drives us crazy, drives us mad. We are bitten and smitten. We sigh for it, die for it; lovers shot and pierced by Cupid's arrow, maimed yet sustained by the lure of love. No neurochemical analysis explains its unquantifiable emotions; no neuropsychological investigation locates its source. Because dying of a broken heart is not just a fictional analogy, but a physiological actuality often observed in the swift death of an elderly couple, the one after the other. This is love.

Love is complex beyond comprehension. It attracts and attaches itself to a vast affective range. It is 'many splendid things';

it is the sacrifice of the soldier, the skill of a surgeon, the courage of the firefighter, the compassion of the nurse. It is celebrating the success of another. It is friendship when times are bad.

Love is sitting by a hospital bed. It is the drawing by a child left on the pillow for a parent. It is an apology. It is words unspoken. It is forging a Valentine's card for a schoolboy to show his friends in school.

Love is grieving a lover. It is letting go. It is loving, sexual intimacy. For some, love is celibacy, choosing a way of life that serves other people.

Love is deep passion between a man and a woman. It is the moment a mother looks in the eyes of her newborn, looks at the father of her child. It is young love. It is 'old' love.

Love is not the battered woman arriving at the refuge. It is not pornography. It is not the broken man cast aside, not cruelty or infidelity. It is not the one-night stand. Love is not the abused child; the infant scarred by a parental blow; the self-loathing of the schoolgoer cornered in the playground, the text message of hate, the street assault.

There are a profusion of psychological descriptions but a scarcity of solutions for loss of love. If we are alive and have thrived in life so far, it is because someone at some time has loved us enough.

How are we loved? Let us count the ways. Every day.

VANITY

From 1999 to 2005, the number of women who would surgically alter their appearance has doubled. From 10 per cent in 1999, recent research commissioned by the Harley Medical Group has found that as many as 20 per cent of Irish women consider cosmetic surgery today.

What motivates women to elect to have surgery, to voluntarily choose the rigours and risks of anaesthetic, scalpel and other somewhat non-aesthetic procedures to alter their appearance? What do they wish to change? Why and for whom do they wish to change? What pressure persuades people to alter their physical and psychological lives?

For it is not just the body that is changed by surgery. There are psychological motivations and consequences to altering one's appearance. And it is rarely just to change the body that people elect to have cosmetic procedures. From the psychological perspective, motivations can include obsessive perfectionism, low self-esteem, poor body image, delusions of deformity, sensitivity to change, need for attention, control issues and fear of ageing. Or motivation may arise from the perceived coercion of one's social group, a perception of cultural requirements for a particular appearance or for social success, or fear of partner loss through rejection and replacement by younger, firmer, more beautiful women.

Additionally, there are unrealistic media representations of womanhood: Lara Croft-type configurations of the human figure invite women to endure body alterations far removed from what nature either intended or can sustain in a healthy body. Body fashions such as breast enhancement, butt enlargement (whatever happened to does my bum look big in this?) and pursuit of the body beautiful entail liposuction, abdominoplasty, breast augmentation, eye-bag removal, lip enlargement, uplifts and face lifts. Whatever we have it seems we want to change it to bigger, better, smaller, firmer and younger. Soon we will all look ten years younger or ten years older, so that the ten-year-old can be twenty and the forty-year-old thirty and women will have no ages outside those ranges if our statistics on the cosmetically challenged are anything to go by.

The research shows that the most sought-after procedure for over half of Irish women is breast uplift or enlargement. Figure-shaping fat removal and tummy-tucks are popular in the 25–44 age bracket. Almost one quarter of us favour Botox or other wrinkle-eradicating solutions and non-surgical laser hair and thread vein removal are regular treatments.

This is not even to factor in the fortune we spend on cosmetics. Think of lipstick, lip-fix and lip-gloss, eye shadows, eye shaders, liners and definers, eyebrow tint and mascara, face bronzers and blushers, body exfoliators and accentuators, tans and foundations in several skin tones with sun-damage-diminishing factors. What about mousses and moisturisers, camouflage and coverage, tints and rinses, highlights and lowlights, perfumes, powders and polishes, manicures and pedicures, waxes and depilators, hair gels, sculptors and sprays?

Then there is the paraphernalia prescribed by obsessive body beautiful seekers: the lean, mean machines of gym and swim, of workout and burn, aerobics, food phobics and culinary cautions that make the enjoyment of a plate of chips or a simple doughnut an occasion of serious cosmetic sin. Soon we may be banished to scoffers' quarters in the nether regions of public buildings for the consumption of non-prescribed food. When sugar fixes are required, we may be subjected to sanctimonious social scrutiny outdoors.

This is not to denigrate healthy living or the normal desire for good appearance. Of course the capacity to alter post-accident injury or deformity enhances the physical and psychological quality of life for those who require it. Understandable, too, is the wish to alter a psychologically distressing unsightly facial or physical feature. And what woman would not augment appearance with some careful cosmetics?

But is the easy availability of cosmetic alteration an individual choice or a collective pressure? The world of each age group has the potential to divide into those that have or have not had cosmetic surgery with confusing consequences. For example, because of those who are chronologically fifty and cosmetically forty, those who naturally look younger will henceforth stand accused of secret cosmetic change. It is a no-win situation for women. For if we alter everyone, we retain everyone in a bizarre arrest of time and denial of reality. How on earth did age-appropriate appearance become a social disease? How have we constructed new categories of psychological distress by this fixation on appearance?

Because there are many whose requests for cosmetic surgery are psychological in origin, who may continue surgery until they acquire a visage devoid of personal expression other than the raised brows of permanent surprise, the stressed appearance of stretched skin, pugilists' lips and personality erasure. The prevalence of depression, of anorexia nervosa and bulimia and body dysmorphic disorder (BDD) are not unrelated to our obsessive preoccupation with how we look.

Of course, the search for beauty is not new. Nor is the belief that if one were only more symmetrical of face, finer of feature, slighter of body, tinier of foot, more elongated, curvaceous, attractive or cute, one would live happily ever after. Shades of the 'ugly sisters' trying to squeeze sweaty, unsightly, enormous feet into the glass slipper pursue us. Women have been reared on fear of ugliness. After all, it was Cinderella, the innately elegant, tiny-toed waif who, on short acquaintance, beguiled the prince with her beauty.

Only Beauty could alter the Beast, transmogrify frogs and out-wit ugly witches. As for Snow White, every older woman at some point empathises with the expensively clad, carefully manicured, meticulously coiffed, bejewelled yet jealous gorgon consulting her 'mirror, mirror on the wall' in the vain hope that she has some-how managed to outwit the savage facial ravages of time. Women understand that wicked woman's desire, if not to be 'the fairest of them all' then at least not to be totally invisible, outshone by the younger, firmer, more beautiful reflections of her former self. Mirrors are strange things. They reflect not what they see, but what we see.

Therein lies the problem. Comparison. Beauty is firmly in the eye of the beholder. Different climates, cultures and epochs have different definitions of what a beautiful woman should be. Art galleries are replete with diverse definitions of human beauty. If each era has conformed to what culture dictated, ours is the only era when we have had the capacity to chemically or surgically alter our shape and size and every aspect of our being. The Ugly Duckling becomes a Swan on reality TV as women are publicly cloned.

Our relationship with age is ambivalent. We seek to be older while we are young and younger when we are older and it is only in grand old age that we proudly declare just how wonderfully old we are. So as plastic surgery turns children into women and women into adult Barbies, the question is who will succumb to surgery and who will succumb to age in all its beauteous indentations, with facial etchings of experience affirming real existence and unafraid to affirm that this life has been lived.

JUSTICE

'The world is still deceived with ornament. In law, what plea so tainted and corrupt but being seasoned with a gracious voice obscures the show of evil'.

William Shakespeare

Justice preoccupies child and philosopher alike. The importance of 'fairness' is evident in the meticulous manner in which children demand that it be demonstrated in every detail. Fairness is required in the pouring of drinks and the distribution of sweets. It is demanded by the democracy of 'turn taking'. Everyone is entitled to a turn, to fair and equal time playing with a designated toy, to equivalent treats and to identical regard in the eyes of parents, teachers and authority figures.

Parents must not have favourites, teachers must not have 'pets': the age at which one is allowed privileges must be the age at which siblings and peers acquired these rights. Life does not have to be perfect: adversity is acceptable provided it is equal. When fairness is flouted the universe is at risk. Injustice is always unacceptable.

In school, a group must not be punished for the wrongdoing of an individual, unfair advantage must not be given to one student above another, praise must be awarded on merit, not on whim, and the consistent, impartial application of rules must be seen to be adhered to. Vigilantes with regard to the administration of justice by adults, young people are quick to observe and abhor any arbitrariness or prejudice in adult behaviour.

Injustice is unpalatable to all age groups. It confuses the child, angers the adolescent, appals the adult and outrages those who have seen its calamitous consequences too many times in a lifetime. This is because they know the many human systems in which injustice may locate itself and 'justify' its lodging.

Some injustices are inequalities experienced by sections of society because of the circumstances of disadvantage of their birth: their gender, skin colour, mental capacity, physical ability, age, wealth and the unwillingness of the surrounding society to challenge unequal treatment based on these facts.

Other injustices may arise randomly, by simply being in the wrong place at the wrong time; by being unable to prove one's victimhood or by finding that there is no adequate legal redress for what one has suffered in an unprovoked attack upon oneself or on one's family. Being the recipient of such an injustice is more than an emotion. It is excruciatingly visceral. It invades the human psyche with the sharpest and most lancing cut. Depending on the severity of the injustice, life may ever after be divided mentally between the time before and after the unjust event.

The experience of injustice alters the perception of oneself, of the safety of the world, the security of life and the belief that wrongs inflicted will be put right. Injustice destroys justice because it destroys belief in justice. It destroys the notion of justice as something more than an activity or an act but as a powerful principle at work in the universe.

For many, receiving justice within the legal system may seem to depend on the capriciousness of circumstances, the existence of witnesses, the admissibility of evidence, and the rigour, laxity, absence, provision or revision of legislation to deal with that particular crime in the jurisdiction in which a person becomes a victim of that crime.

For some, what is perceived as 'judicial injustice' is a crime upon the crime: a further defilement after rape and an insult that exceeds the original assault. This structural 'injustice' seems to seek to rationalise the crime, construct victims as consensual or complicit in their suffering and construe as inadmissible that which any rational person would regard as relevant to a case. In so doing it discredits the reality of victims and fails to redress their hurt. For to go to court is to petition for justice. A case dismissed is a person dismissed if justice is not served. When the rules of law excessively challenge the right to justice, a review of legal structures is required.

People tend to believe in the power of justice until they have an experience that refutes that belief. What makes injustice particularly painful for those who experience it is not relinquishment of a belief in fair redress, but that belief in fairness itself is lost.

Clinically, the emotions and behaviours consequent upon perception of grave injustice are many. Injustice may bring a need to wail with primitive, howling outrage. It may show itself in scorched receding eyes that will not recount what has occurred. It may speak loudly, livid with determination to redress the wrong. It may be barely audible, unable to articulate the depth of the despair. Sometimes it will regress to childlike questioning of how such unfairness could occur or be allowed. Sometimes it arms itself with anger, unrestrained, to revenge what others will not 'right'. It is all action and immobility, all words and silence, all weeping and hysteria, all reality and illusion.

Sometimes it chokes in indignation. Sometimes it sobs with frustration. Sometimes it closes in upon itself, emerging in depression. Other times it defends itself in denial. Sometimes it pretends it never happened. Sometimes it is consumed with nothing else.

The psychological consequences of injustice usually present as post-traumatic symptoms and with time and sensitive intervention are amenable to psychotherapy. Victims of crime should seek support.

ETHICAL
AND
SOCIAL ISSUES

Introduction

Ethics are frequently treated as if they are abstract, Utopian concepts that are unattainable. One might be forgiven for thinking them to be idealised aspirations, impossible objectives and rhetorical reassurances, rather than having anything to do with ordinary life as lived. Much occurs in Ireland that suggests that economic imperatives outweigh ethical dimensions when decisions are being made and that chicanery is secretly admired.

As poet Czeslaw Milosz reminds us, 'The hierarchy of ethical values is easily overturned and its ranks reassembled.' Could it be that expediency supersedes principles, that profit supersedes honesty and that care and compassion are conveniently contained in ethical codes rather than enacted in compassionate care? Could it be that the potential for personal profit makes people compromise their ethical principles? Could it be that vested interests are privileged, that power, status and money talk louder than vulnerability, indignity and poverty? Because despite extraordinary individual altruism, personal philanthropy and much ordinary kindness shown by many, many people in the service of others in this country, there is an equally perturbing public tolerance for unethical practice that goes across the social, economic and political echelons of Irish life, almost as if, in some pathological way, the rogue is revered.

Where are ethical values if older people who are needy, incapacitated and unable to defend themselves are neglected, exploited and abused? What do we do when there are deep ideological differences between people about bioethics, about life and death, about when we die and how we die, who decides, who assists and who resists any attempt to hasten the end of those who are terminally ill? Whose ethics prevail when we are direct targets for invasive marketing? And how can we even think about anything when we live our lives in places where construction noise never stops? For despite major manifestos, plenty of policy, reams of rhetoric and myriad mission statements by politicians, people are not protected from noise pollution.

Ethics are an integral part of research: but is research always ethical? Elaborate mechanisms for attending to physical and mental health are devised, but are these new models mere replicas of traditional religious practice? What questions about our national psyche remain unanswered and does our colonial past help to explain our postcolonial ethical vacuity, or is that just another narrative of blame?

Attempting to explore ethical and social issues may be defeating, for where does one begin and where to end? How can issues be raised without morale being lowered? How can stridency be avoided while making sturdy points that represent the strong feelings people have about these issues? I cannot tell. These are the fingerprints of a living society, not static matters, and the way one writes today may change tomorrow, as life changes, as laws are enacted and as, despite all, civilisation marches forward rather than back.

Shocked by
What We Knew

---

*'Ambition drove many men to become false; to have
one thought locked in the breast, another ready on the
tongue.'*

Sallust

Shocked. Shocking. We are shocked by media revelations, for example, by the undercover uncovering of the reality of elder abuse. We are shocked to learn the carelessness with which we 'care' for others. News channels are clogged with our concern. Airwaves reverberate with our amazement. Formal declarations of 'shock' have rung out throughout the land, tolling the end to corrupt practice, to confusions in communication, to administrative inaccuracy, to unintentional misappropriation of monies, to inadvertent misallocation of files and to undesirable dereliction of duty.

The rhetoric of refutation and rebuff has begun. No ricochets of remorse. Not a *mea culpa* in sight. Instead a plethora of platitudes: the reading of reports, the commissioning of inquiries, the implementation of inspections, the examination of facts, the calling of meetings, the drafting of legislation, the enactment of regulations. The full rigours of obfuscation can commence.

The truth, if truth be identifiable on this island, is that we are not shocked by what we have learned about abuse of the elderly in this society. We are shocked by what we knew. Shocked at us, ourselves: shocked by who we are and what we have become. We are shocked that we did nothing. Shocked we do not do enough. Shocked that economic imperatives, sustainability of public finances and ideologies of self have superseded social objectives and community concern.

Who can say they did not know the inadequacies of services? A *Prime Time* programme exposed us all. This was not consciousness-raising. It was conscience rousing of the most challenging kind. We did not know? We did not know the elderly were vulnerable, could be victims of physical neglect, emotional isolation, financial exploitation, callous coercion, physical assault, bruising, battering and sexual abuse?

Who did not know that the vulnerable are always prey for the unscrupulous: the greedy, the cold, the calculating, the unfeeling, the opportunistic? Who did not know that provisions were inadequate, pensions a problem, poverty a reality, frailty a fact and that deceptions of the dependent, the demented, the dying are inevitable when institutions are not inspected?

We did not know the elderly could be robbed? Subventions stolen by the state? Self-respect denied? Have we not seen them stretched on trolleys, shuffling their indignant way, half clad, to nearby toilets, hoping that on return they will not have lost the least of their entitlements: a public plinth on which to lie? We never held a nose, averted eyes or crept uncomfortably from the defilements of dependent age? Let no more doubt obtain. We have put our hands inside the wounds, followed cameras into the cavities of neglect. We know.

The psychology of ageing is well documented. The neglect of the aged is not. High on the list are physical constraint, the indignity of being dirty, the desperation of being thirsty, the emptiness of feeling hungry, the helplessness of being sore, the frustration of waiting for food to be cut, an object that has fallen to be retrieved and assistance to go to the bathroom in time. There is the suffering of being shouted at, being punished for existing, small ailments neglected, major medical needs denied. There may be indeterminate waiting for personal purchases; sweets, cigarettes, whiskey, newspapers and contact with friends. What is it like to be denied choice of food, access to snacks, to self-determination about waking and sleeping, to options in activities or the right to seek professional advice personally? All these neglects are possible and we know that they occur.

Because we have valued 'economy' more than care, and words like 'burden' have frequently been heard. We have left carers unsupported, slave labour to fiscal state sustainability, impoverished by their concern for their husbands or wives, their mothers or fathers, all those who are dependent upon them whom they love. Their love is exploited; they are weighed down by duty, lacking regard, with little respite, poor recognition, absent or insulting remuneration, reaching desperation with options unimaginable.

The controversy between Lawrence Kohlberg's ethics of rights and Carol Gilligan's ethics of care is relevant. The ethics of rights and justice are abstract: they proclaim what we should hypothetically do. The ethics of care are concrete, concerned with what we actually do and our personal responsibility in the process. We have heard much of the former and need more of the latter.

In a radio transmission in 1939, Franklin D. Roosevelt reportedly said 'repetition does not transform a lie into a truth'. It would seem that he was wrong. Repetition is the new rhetoric of 'ethics', the ethics of rhetoric having outgrown the need for such senile sensibilities as accuracy. Hyperbole replaces honesty, oratory replaces reality, where the truth is the said and the said is spun, woven with tiny truth treads sufficient to satisfy.

But somewhere at this moment, a fading voice calls, again, and again, for the newspaper dropped on the floor out of reach. Who will pick that up?

To Tell or
Not to Tell

To be a child is to be the recipient of a wild array of ambiguous adult messages. Many of us will remember the confusing contradictions inherent in these adult instructions. 'Tell the truth/don't tell tales' was one of the more pernicious adult imperatives, leaving children like goldfish opening and shutting their mouths in circular double-bound confusion about whether telling was worse than not telling and in what circumstances.

Indeed, one of the preoccupations of childhood was cracking the complex code of adult communication: a task that required serious eavesdropping on adult exchanges, acute observation of the consequences when siblings or friends breached this indecipherable code, trial and error experiments and finally acquiring the assistance of other citizens of childhood who were more advanced in circumventing adult double-bind communications.

These early mental acrobatics probably account for our unique Irish communicative patterns of peeling back linguistic layers of messages before arriving at meaning – in other words, finding what we mean behind what we really mean underneath what we really, really mean. This is the same repetitive psychological rumination that forces us to ask 'are you sure?' several times before we will accept that someone 'really' does not want the proffered biscuit with the offered cup of tea.

But if asking is complex, telling is fraught with danger. This is because we remember that attached to telling or tale-telling in childhood were words like 'snitch' and 'sniveller' and every telltale was a 'tattler': a sly, sneaky sucker-upper despised by both adult and child. Worse, the history of Ireland as taught in times past was imbued with the duplicity of the 'informer'– that most treacherous, seditious, unscrupulous sneak whose perfidy occupied chapters and chapters of prescribed text.

In school whole classes stood rigid, gaze avoidant at requests to 'identify the culprit' while wishing that the culprit would just 'own up' before group retribution was unfairly required. Today many people suffer a similar anxiety in any situation where they may have to 'tell tales' – the apprehension generated by past interrogations engendering a present angst at investigatory, transparency or accountability practices.

Perhaps that message from the past has permeated the present. Perhaps the childhood dilemma of 'to tell or not to tell' made its bi-directional way into the adult psyche, so that ethical ineptitude ensued. Perhaps the message that emerged was 'to do is fine' but 'to get caught a crime' and to stay silent, to 'turn a blind eye' to avoid conflict and confrontation are psychologically safer and pragmatically preferable.

Whatever the ambiguity of the past, the present is clear: many people suffer from a pathological inability to initiate a complaint or to answer direct questions that uncover corruption in the workplace. The fear of 'informing' runs deep, even when such information is important for their own psychological health or that of their work colleagues. The moral milieu that facilitates corruption in the first place usually includes an emotional embargo on 'telling'. This surreptitious injunction first confuses and then silences new entrants to the organisation who may be part of what they observe before they observe what they are part of. Ethical exposé is not encouraged.

It is not easy to leave a workplace in precarious times, to leave a permanent, pensionable position. Men in particular are often trapped by being the sole financial support for their family or by their sensitivity to the primacy of this prescribed role. To leave means finding alternative employment, confronting possible rejection, encountering issues of age, of relevant qualifications, of securing a position of equal status and acquiring a reference from one's current employer while the reason for leaving has to be either hidden or given. Many people also describe the terrible fear that, having remained in a post while they were aware of unethical practices in that workplace, they will be accused of collusion, will share culpability or will be made the scapegoat when the sorry situation is finally revealed.

From a psychological perspective, each new public disclosure of individual callousness, professional mismanagement, institutional corruption or organisational dishonesty excavates and re-creates the emotions of that childhood ethical quandary 'to tell or not to tell', to whom, how and in what way and with what consequences.

The mental health sequelae of silence are considerable, including feelings of unhappiness, helplessness and hopelessness and there is a high risk of depression depending on the seriousness of the situation. People experience anxiety every single day: apprehension in anticipation of the work day ahead, anger at being an uninvited, inadvertent witness to what is wrong, fear of the consequence of divulging: of being disbelieved, challenged, invalidated or ridiculed or of experiencing organisational retribution for being the 'informer', the 'whistle-blower', the disloyal defector.

While society excoriates its past, excavates its practices, uncovers corruptions, divulges discrepancies and trawls through tribunals, investigations and interrogations, psychological recuperation for those who have been caught in the tangled webs of others' deceit may require the catharsis of telling the tale and receiving unequivocal respect as informants to an ethical society rather than informers.

Bioethics: End
and Ending
of Life

Bioethical issues are at the forefront of public debate. When they concern the inception or cessation of life, anxiety is intensified, debate is deepened and ideological differences can become dogmatically divisive.

Indeed, they may become so emotionally laden that people regress into positions that admit no other conviction but their own. This is because life and death decisions, personal liberty and interpersonal responsibility, the right to choose and choosing what is right, self-determination or social consensus are extraordinarily ethical, complex and crucial at this time.

One critical ethical issue is euthanasia, or assisted suicide, a topic gathering momentum as individual countries face the debate on whether legalising euthanasia means legalising human murder or legalising humane, merciful release for dying citizens from the indignities of the final stages of debilitating illness.

We are at our most vulnerable before birth and before death. It is at entry and exit to human existence that we depend upon others for our safety: the security of our journey into or out of this world, the inviolability of our human rights and the definitions of human viability. Therefore, who, what, why, when and how we ourselves or others decide our fate at these critical junctures will determine whether we may live and when we will die.

Those in favour of assisted suicide say that a person has the right to choose the moment and manner of death if death is imminent, inevitable and otherwise likely to be one of personal indignity, prolongation of pain or the misery felt by family members witnessing the suffering of their loved one. They speak about dying on one's own terms, about painless mercy killing being a merciful release from life. This is death with dignity, they say.

Is it not cruel to prolong the agonies of life's end: to maintain people in pervasive vegetative states, breathing cadavers in incapacity and immobility? If animals are put out of their misery, do not humans deserve equal compassion? They say that a citizen has the right to die with dignity. They believe that one is competent to make 'living will' choices during life about later death. Death should be permitted and assisted.

Those against assisted suicide question the hidden coercion and level of choice a citizen has in a society prepared to use medical means to terminate life. They point to the slippery slope from stringent controls to flexible conditions once we author life and death.

They fear euthanasia becoming a death warrant for the disabled, becoming paediatric euthanasia, then eugenics, then economic valuations of viability. They refute arguments about release from pain, given biotechnological advancements in pain alleviation. They ask whose purpose 'release' truly serves.

Euthanasia is not about dying with dignity; rather, it is another step towards the death of the dignity of life. It is not dying on one's own terms but the terms of a society that may soon permit only the perfect to survive. Citizens have the right to live, to commitment to improving the lives of the terminally ill, not terminating their lives.

Euthanasia may be active, passive, voluntary, involuntary and non-voluntary. These distinctions make its ethical exigencies even more complex and contentious. The difference between carrying out an act that ends life and not acting in a way that prolongs life is central to the argument.

What is described as the 'principle of double effect' suggests that the intention of an act or its omission determines its ethics. Letting life go gently, naturally, providing pain relief, is appropriate palliative care. Intent defines euthanasia.

Many who agree with voluntary euthanasia would not sanction non-voluntary or involuntary euthanasia, because in these situations the person is unable to make a choice or actively does not wish to die.

But it behoves those who believe in voluntary euthanasia to remember that the request for death by a person who is terminally ill may mask unidentified treatable clinical depression. Consider the danger of undiagnosed depression if its symptoms of psychological pain, physical depletion and morbid hopelessness became grounds for assisted suicide. What if treatable depression was dismissed in favour of termination of life? What if our response to the impulse of suicide itself was to assist it? How would 'intolerable pain' be defined and who would have the right to define that? And how many people who are now alive, happily so, would be dead if they were given an out, instead of an anti-depressant, and if they were given 'assistance' to die instead of psychotherapy to assist them to live?

Where would we draw the line between physical suffering, psychological pain, bodily incapacity and mental demise? And what would become of palliative care? Would that be merely an option: surely a compromised choice if others were choosing more immediate departures from life?

The request to die, the so-called 'living will', may reflect loss of the 'will to live', a classic emotion in clinical depression or a psychologically vulnerable time in chronic illness: time of darkest night and lowest ebb. If requests for death are responded to, not by pulling the plug but by providing love, compassion, counselling and care, they may transform into a living will to live.

The desire to die may be a right. Desire is not deed. But promoting the desire to live is the task of mental health professionals, a flexible, supportive medical and social service and richly resourced palliative care.

Health care cannot be morally neutral, nor can health care workers allow legislation to deny them ethical self-governance, however sanitised the terminology. Medicine and murder must be mutually exclusive. We need hospice, not 'hemlock' societies, care, not Kovorkianism, lest we lapse into 'permitting the destruction of life not worthy of life', termination without specific request or the euphemisms of eugenics.

There are dangers when single-case compassion becomes the basis for societal legislation, the danger that as professionals we might, in the words of philosopher Fr Richard John Neuhaus, 'guide the unthinkable on its passage through the debatable on its way to becoming the justifiable until it is finally established as the unexceptional'.

This is why, despite individual cases which must evoke compassion, one cannot subscribe to the 'final solution' of 'assisted suicide' because *all* life is 'worthy of life' and measures of worthiness are not within our authorship.

Investment in living rather than assistance toward death must be preferable. Health care has its own ethical imperatives and obligations: surely working to create ideal conditions for living one's natural life has to be one of them.

OLD AGE
AIN'T NO PLACE
FOR SISSIES

The implication of George Bernard Shaw's statement that 'youth is wasted on the young' is that with age comes perspective, with living learning, with experience wisdom and with time an appreciation of time's passage. Youth second time around would be appreciated. It would be savoured rather than squandered.

How ironic to know the value of what one possessed only when ownership has ended, to recognise the riches of being young when youth has passed, to spot the pitfalls from their depths or know which roads to choose having chosen otherwise.

'If I knew then what I now know' is the frequent regretful refrain of age. What wisdom would have shaped our lives if we had been concurrently bestowed with youth's time and age's wisdom? Mutually exclusive, the wisdom of age is not the gift of the young and the timelessness of youth is not bequeathed to old age. Life is lived without rehearsals.

Of course, for some lucky individuals fortune and chance combine to gift them with what they would have wished for in life anyway. Serendipity sends them to careers they treasure. Happenstance produces life partners of love, commitment and integrity and children who find happiness in their lives. Life's hurdles are placed beside appropriate supports. Misfortune does not visit maliciously.

Other people, who are less fortunate, encounter hardships. Hurt by hard luck, hardened by hurt, time is not kind to them. But there is no return to youth to begin again. Some people respond to their own misfortune by addressing the inequalities of their era. They challenge social inequities and become ardent adversaries against injustice. If they cannot return to the past or change their own lives, they can at least alter the future for later generations. Each generation in its own way contributes to the past, the present and the future.

Individuals also assert their entitlement to make their own mistakes. 'Learning the hard way' is the colloquialism for regretful retrospect when in later life some discover that their 'elders' had helpful advice, had they been listened to. Conversely, others who heeded warnings from a more cautious generation wish they had not done so, that they had listened to their own hearts and dared to do what is now undoable. The future cannot be foretold. Each person must plan his or her life path based on the information they have at that time.

The question is, then, how can we at any life stage learn from the present, forestall the future and plan for what lies ahead? This is not just a question for the young. It is a question for everyone. It is an absolute necessity for those who are within shouting distance of old age.

In a world that is fearful of age rather than reverential before its wisdom, dismissive of its needs rather than respectful of its rights, disdainful of its abilities and indifferent to its contribution, it is time for those who are older to plan for the future. The paucity of support systems, the breakdown of health care facilities and the revelations about the unchallenged, exploitative, opportunistic, callous and cruel treatment suffered by many older people in nursing homes makes this planning essential.

The deficit description of age omits the positive acquisitions that age brings. It dismisses the important, different and extensive abilities of older people. This deficit model ignores the research which shows the important contribution older people make in society, the fact that many are more flexible thinkers, able to debate many sides of an argument, that they may have greater appreciation of social change and acceptance of the multiple perspectives and points of view that people hold.

Older people often have a talent for tolerating ambiguities and a capacity for complex thinking because they understand that few issues are black and white. They have witnessed personalities, communities and ideologies rise and fall. They are aware of how short life is and how insignificant many of the preoccupations of youth in the greater scheme of things are.

There is realism about the future that comes with age: an understanding that certain cognitive, physical and self-help capacities may alter. There is stoicism when confronted by loss. There is humour and kindly amusement at the swaggering, strutting and striving sometimes shown by younger people.

Being older means that posturing has no place, that one has abandoned superficiality and that one has lived through and adapted to many shifts in society. It means that there is nothing to prove. Survival in a changing world is proof of the talent and tenacity of age.

It is from this clarity and autonomy when one is in this non-dependent, assertive older age that plans for the future should be made. The body does not always keep pace with the mind and the decline in physical ability is one of the aggravating grievances of advanced age to be catered for, preferably before it occurs. It makes sense to get one's financial affairs in order to ensure that one has physical comforts, social outlets, intellectual interests and leisure activities for the future.

Acquiring e-mail and Internet skills ensures that one will never be deprived of communication or information about world affairs. Purchasing the technology that allows enjoyment of one's preferred music, films and books ensures control over future leisure time regardless of physical strength.

Many people prepare practically by planning maintenance-free homes and gardens and by installing the requirements for a less physically able time in advance. This means having phones with large digits, stored numbers, redial and speaker options, having panic buttons, alarm systems and security cameras at buzzer-operated doors.

It means having implements to assist lifting, to aid opening bottles, jars and tins. It is important to have apparatus to retrieve fallen objects and to facilitate mobility. Some people invest in a downstairs bedroom or install chair lifts, accessible showers and baths, high-placed electrical sockets, adjustable beds and remote controls for all appliances.

Provision for the future includes good legal advice now about what you wish to happen in the event of becoming physically less able, psychiatrically ill or generally unable to cope in the future. Decisions about whom to trust with power of attorney should that become necessary and a will that stipulates that it cannot be changed without the presence of certain specified people is important to ensure that coercion by the unscrupulous cannot occur.

It makes sense to check out protected private housing for 'the elderly', properties that have maintenance staff and access to nursing staff if needed and to visit nursing homes to decide where one might wish to be if necessary later in life.

Planning for the future liberates the present. It is then time to 'live it up', time to show that while 'youth may be wasted on the young', age is not wasted on the aged. This is the time to do all the things that previously there was no time to do, visit the places one always wished to see, develop the friendships that will sustain one into the future, savour each moment in a way never possible in the past.

'Old age ain't no place for sissies,' Bette Davis once said. She was right. It takes courage to be older. Age is admirable. Age is an accomplishment. It is an assertion of adaptability, recognition of resolve, determination of doggedness and a celebration of assertiveness. It tells us there is a future. It assures us that if we cannot turn back 'time', we can certainly challenge it and make each moment count.

Bet there ain't no sissies amongst the older people you are privileged to know.

SENSE OF
HUMOUR

Most psychologists will know about the man who approaches, with great respect, a young woman sitting alone at a table in the college canteen to ask her if she would like a coffee, to which she shouts, in a very loud voice, 'No I will not sleep with you.'

Embarrassed, he slinks away, but is approached by her several minutes later with an apology and the explanation that she is a psychology student researching reactions to embarrassing situations, whereupon he shouts out in the loudest voice, 'Okay, okay, €100 then.'

While this may not be the funniest story recounted, it does contain some of the essential ingredients that make humour objectively funny and appealingly reassuring. Just what these ingredients are is always difficult to define, but some level of self-recognition is crucial: that is, having the capacity to imagine oneself either as one of the participants or one of the onlookers in the story. Ambivalent responses are common: for example, empathy with the person who is embarrassed yet enjoyment of the power held by the person who caused the embarrassment.

A further ingredient in the majority of jokes is that the tables are turned: the victim becomes the victor. This ingredient in the story above delights us, because the man who was initially the unwitting subject of the experiment surprisingly subjects the experimenter to her own experiment. We are not told her reaction. That would alter the impact and destroy the joke. Instead our imaginations are left chuckling at the possibilities. Indignation on her part would be inappropriate, for had she not expected others to succumb to her research? Anger would be inexcusable, for if the research is such that it would anger another, then should it be conducted in the first place? Embarrassment should certainly occur if her own research design and methodology are valid and reliable in scientific terms. Otherwise her experiment has failed. Justice is done, but done with humour. The reprisal does not exceed the original act.

Humour must be credible, not cruel. Sharp, not spiteful. It must be of the 'ouch' variety, an epiphany wherein a truth is revealed, a revelation takes place for the characters in the story and for us as the listeners to the account. A further dimension to jokes is that those listening to them recognise some aspect of themselves or other people they know.

Jokes must contain something quirky about life that has not previously been articulated in this way. Jokes are funny because they expose the inexpressible, express the inexplicable and reveal that which we usually conceal. They say the unsayable, promise the impossible and lead us where we normally fear to tread.

In this way jokes invite vicarious incursions into the terrains of taboo. Those life and death experiences we fear most, those things that irritate, infuriate, confuse, intimidate, anguish or embarrass us, are laughed at. That which we dread is said. Things that are not discussed in normal circumstances, nor in polite circles, suddenly are commented upon in the company of others whose reactions we can observe. This is why so many jokes about death, sex, religion, race, politics, power and complex relationships abound. Jokes are about life.

Stories and jokes negotiate the most intricate psychological balances. Too close to reality is uncomfortable, too distant is irrelevant. There is a delicate and deliberate distance between danger and safety, between respect and irreverence. What is required is a jibe that is nonetheless just a joke. Such storytelling regresses us to the thrill of challenging 'authority', breaking a rule and awaiting the consequences. This is why children cover their mouths, whispering in guilty giggles at the lamentably lavatorial vulgarities that typify many first incursions into the silly side of humour.

With the achievement of adulthood it is expected that trite tastelessness and salaciousness will be replaced by appropriate acumen and social accuracy, which is why a comedian outside his culture is on uncertain psychological soil and can inadvertently offend to the deepest degree. Nonetheless, an element of hand-over-mouth infantile tension remains an essential ingredient of humour. That is, it works well when it dares to say or do that which in ordinary circumstances cannot be said or done. There is a guilty edge to laughter when we have crossed, imaginatively, a boundary that we would not dream of approaching in our everyday lives.

Jokes depend upon the teller, the audience and the tale. They depend upon the context in which they are told, the manner in which they are told, whether they are unexpected vignettes or sequential sketches recounted in the course of joke-telling sessions. Amusement is also evoked by witty conversational interjections, by particularly apt stories and even by those deliberate extracts from the joke-teller's repertoire of tales, which are usually prefaced by 'have you heard the one about'.

For a joke has a short life. It may be enjoyed but once. Thereafter amusement comes from witnessing the reaction of other people to hearing the joke. This in itself is an interesting human generosity evoked by jokes. They not only provide happiness in us when we hear them and cheerfulness in us when we tell them, but our enjoyment is extended by anticipating and watching for that moment of amused realisation in another person when they 'get the joke'.

But a joke is more than humour. There may be profundity behind profanity, truth beneath trivia and lessons in laughter. Take the story that began this article. We are amused by allegory, not least in the parable it provides for every psychologist who remembers that ethically the first question to be asked before undertaking any research investigation is: how would I feel if this were done to me? Funny, that.

TIRED OF BEING
A TARGET

Is anyone irritated? Is anyone really annoyed with the wasted time and energy expended daily deleting unwanted e-mails, disposing of uninvited junk through the letterbox or 'opting out' of direct marketing harassment? This latest pestering is particularly irritating. Why should people have to put in writing their desire NOT to receive information that they never requested? Why should they have to opt out of something they never opted into in the first place? Why? Because as legislation on data protection tries to control the avalanche of advertising abuse inflicted upon ordinary citizens, those who make money by exploiting the contact details of their clients (or should that read the information they provide to associate organisations?) try to find ways around it. How do they do this? They ask you to opt out. Of course, offering you the option to opt out is the ideal way to ensnare you, because in this hurried, busy, information-overloaded world, chances are you won't find the time to do so. And if you don't opt out, you opt in.

The literature implies that there is a time limit to your choice to be or not to be a recipient of all the 'latest information about products'. Unless you register your desire *not* to receive the information you never requested by a specified date, then you will continue to be sent it. However, if you have the time to read further into the brochure (and who has time for this?) it emerges that you can opt out at any time by writing to the address provided. This is because that is your legal right, and so that information must be hidden somewhere in the blurb amongst the other bumf you don't have time to read, telling you how to do what you don't have time to do, and should not have to do in the first place, in this rather insane society we call consumerist.

Furthermore, if you try to opt out, you may find that the freephone number doesn't work, there is no addressed envelope amongst the literature with which to make a written reply and no e-mail option offered by which to register one's choice. Would it be paranoid to suggest that e-mail would provide immediate written proof that one does not want to hear from them?

Of course, even if freephone numbers do not work, there is usually an alternative number that one can ring at one's own expense and hold, while options for company 'products' are conveyed numerically, so that you play a concerto of digital digits until you reach the crescendo of a human voice, a customer server, nay, a 'server of valued customers' who 'checks the system' and informs you that yes, indeed, 'the system is temporarily down'. Now when did a phone become a 'system', and a broken phone something 'temporarily down'?

Temporarily down is exactly how the 'valued customer' feels after any foray into the 'smarmspeak' of marketing. For who has not heard the slick salesman cajole a young couple who have just purchased a new couch into buying rather expensive unnecessary insurance for it, given that the product should have its own warranty and their house insurance covers the unforeseen? Who has not retched emotionally at the manner in which genuine complaint is met with a litany of stock, solicitous phrases, none of which simply includes 'I'm sorry'? Who has not listened to the glib gibberish delivered by the unethical to the uninformed that intimidates them into acquiescing to the unacceptable when they have been deprived of their rights? Who is fed up with being called a 'valued customer' while simultaneously being demeaned?

This is not a trivial issue, this irritability of customers confronted by the profanity of consumerism at its most intrusive. This is a health issue. It is a genuine stress on an already 'overloaded system', to borrow the parlance of postmodernity. Stress arises when people feel incapable of coping with the demands made upon them. There are health hazards in 'smarmspeak' and having to protect oneself constantly from direct marketing hits. This new spate of stress by syntax and small print that attempts to circumvent data protection legislation by befuddling the overburdened is yet another example of stealth stress. It is wrong. Don't call us, we'll call you should surely be a consumer's right.

As people become the targets of more and more missiles from the marketing world – mobile text ads, Blackberry bombardment, e-mail intrusion, twenty-four-hours-a-day contactability and the rather persistent insistence that the customer do all the work and pay for the privilege – they become weary of life itself.

Long before the 'Tiger economy' there was a Dominican nun in Dublin renowned for her warning to generations of school children that 'the Devil goes around like a roaring lion seeking whom he may devour'. They laughed. They didn't know she was prophetic.

The Noise

that

Never Stops

How do you drive someone over the edge? How do you make them dread each waking day knowing that at least eleven hours of torture may await them? Well, the answer is by noise. Legal noise, building noise, noise that never stops. This is the noise of progress and development.

Noise is a serious threat to our physical and mental health. And it is getting LOUDER. Noise is measured in decibels: conversation averages about 60 decibels. Noise reaches painful proportions around 120–130 decibels. Over certain decibel limits, people become stressed, frustrated and irritated, preoccupied by the noise and unable to tolerate its continuance. They become unable to concentrate. They become obsessed with the cessation of the invasion of noise. They say the noise is 'killing' them.

Environmental, pollutant noise has an ever-increasing variety of sources and sounds, but its volume does not necessarily predict the degree of 'annoisance' it will cause. This is because of the type, tone, frequency, pitch, 'contours' and 'footprints' of the noise.

Adaptable as we humans are, we often do not register residual or general ambient noise that is familiar and continuous, such as toneless heating systems – until they stop! We register what we require. Increases or decreases in noise alert us. Impulsive noises startle us: the brief, abrupt backfiring motorbike. Low-frequency power plant noise is intrusive. Annoying tones make us tense: motors, grinding gears, noise pounding rhythmically within our heads.

Advances in technology have raised decibel levels in all living contexts, the whirring, whining, slurping, grinding of the machinery of our lives; hum of fridge, whisk of mixer, whoosh of dishwasher, drone of air conditioner, vroom of vacuum cleaner, grind of coffee-maker, the chaotic cacophony of current existence and of our increasingly noisy lives.

Technology has also provided us with more ways to construct buildings. A problem of relatively recent origin is the intensity and extent of home reconstructions, renovations and extensions in former 'leafy suburbs' and peaceful places. In the past, domestic 'development' tended to confine itself to minor home improvements such as the classic garage extension into playroom. These works were of short duration and noise level. The family lived on-site. Work proceeded within family-friendly time.

But all has changed, changed utterly. Today, residential life is under siege from serial, major building. Planning laws have not kept pace. No consideration of the increase in environmental noise is apparent in the oft-quoted legislation of a decade ago. With prohibitive house costs, the trend is to buy a small house and double its size, build another dwelling on any patch of excess garden, convert large homes into apartment blocks and extend backwards, upwards and outwards with projects that may subject neighbours to months and months of excruciating noise.

While planning laws examine individual applications, they do not appear to examine the sequence of building projects in an area or consider noise emission from simultaneous building projects. Conceivably, a family living in a semi-detached in a residential estate could have concurrent building projects conducted legally on either side, behind and in the houses across the road from their home.

The guidelines dictated by developers to government allow building noise between 8 a.m. and 7 p.m. from Monday to Friday and between 8 a.m. and 1 p.m. on Saturdays. This is eleven hours a day, five days a week! This is from morning until night. This is the longed-for lie-in on a Saturday morning. This is the shift worker returning to sleep, the night porter, fireman, factory worker. This is the elderly housebound couple. This is the student studying. This is the new baby, mother and father. This is you. This is me. This is the dissonant demise of the quality of our lives in the interest of progress. This is not okay, not personally, not spiritually, nor physiologically, nor psychologically.

The assessment and management of environmental noise is the responsibility of government. We look to government and its agencies to protect us from environmental hazards. Noise is one of these hazards. Our protection feels minimal. It was reported at the 2003 European Conference on Noise Control that in Western Europe, about 80 million people suffer from noise levels that experts consider unacceptable and that annual financial losses due to environmental noise run to billions.

Here in Ireland, a spokesperson for the Minister for the Environment, Heritage and Local Government says that the position in relation to noise nuisance generally is that a legal remedy is provided under Section 108 of the Environmental Protection Agency Act 1992 and the associated Environmental Protection

Agency Act 1992 (Noise) Regulations, 1994. This makes it possible for an individual to apply to the District Court in respect of noise which gives reasonable cause for annoyance to obtain an order for the reduction, prevention or limitation of the noise. Local authorities can also require measures to be taken to prevent or limit noise. 'This is a simplified low-cost process which does not require help from individual local authorities,' he adds. 'The court charges about €15 to process the action; the use of noise recording equipment is not necessarily required and there is no requirement to be represented in court by a solicitor.' In summary, if it bothers you, prosecute and prove it.

But that means that there is precious little the lone, noise-demented citizen can do. What new mother, what frail diminutive woman, what exhausted man, what stressed student confronts the builder above the noise of the cement mixer to 'notify him, seven days in advance, of intent to bring court proceedings'? What reprieve is there in the intervening seven days, listening dementedly to decibel levels to record their 'unreasonable' discord? And who is the culprit if the building noise is from several simultaneous sources? What person goes into court without objective measurement or the support of a solicitor against the might of construction corporations and at the risk of losing and paying the costs of confronting noise pollution?

Come now, Minister. This is not a solution. This is noisome nonsense. The process is rendered ridiculously risky and sufficiently unwieldy for noise victims to deter them from taking action. Noise just doesn't seem to be taken into account in the granting of planning permission. There appears to be no specified upper noise levels; nothing about the particularly deleterious impact of the startling stop/start noise duets in domestic areas. What decibel restrictions are there? What restrictions regarding duration of intense, invasive noise other than time guidelines? Where is the requirement on builders to forewarn neighbours about particularly disruptive activities? There is no apparent co-ordination on the commencement of building works, nothing to prohibit the commencement of one construction until the completion of another. There is no definition of the proximity within which a new work may not commence while a current one is in progress. There is no apparent reprieve.

There is a saying that only the fish do not know that they live in water. We too have forgotten the 'silence', tranquillity and the peace in which we once lived before road noise and rat running, before road works, gridlock and economic 'growth'. We have forgotten nature's sounds and the delight of silence. A reprieve from noise is our human right. European aspirations, those of CALM, the network of the EU noise initiative on noise emission, recognise the importance of 'quiet areas', the importance of conducting environmental impact studies that recognise that 'no person should be exposed to noise levels which endanger health and quality of life'.

The issue of noise is an issue of public concern, of health and safety. It is one that warrants greater local authority and legislative provision than appears to be available under the current outdated 1994 cited provisions.

The solution does not lie in retributive mechanisms to prosecute builders for making noise, nor in paranoid prowling reading local 'gates' to object to planning applications and thwart good neighbours' attempts to improve their lot. The solution lies in proper planning and noise pollution protections that prohibit the occurrence of noxious noise levels in the first place.

It is time for citizens to make some noise of their own. Time to protest before the world ends, not with a whisper, but a bang.

ATTENDING
RELIGIOUSLY
TO HEALTH

Amongst the many therapeutic interventions that research has found to enhance physical and mental health, one remains remarkably conspicuous by its absence – having a religious belief.

The vast research which correlates religious practice with proactive health practices, physiological healing and psychological reassurance remains primarily ignored in the present phenomenal public discourses about health and illness. This is intriguing, given our current preoccupation with issues of health.

Consider the enormous array of therapies advertised today for every conceivable, and many implausible, psychological problems we allegedly acquire by virtue of being alive. It would seem that we suffer from a medley of mental infirmities we never knew we had until we were told how deleterious their effects were. This extemporaneous list is expanding.

Like hypochondriacs perusing medical dictionaries of symptoms only to discover that they suffer signs of all described diseases, the hypnotic power of the mentally hypothetical has ensnared us in an iatrogenic web. We now, perhaps, believe that we are not, cannot be and will never ever be complete, fulfilled, healed, realised, actualised, authentic, found, recouped, at one with our inner child, ego-esteemed, ontologically secure and satisfied until we have endured the rigours of confronting the 'self', whoever, whatever or how many that/those self-same selves may be.

And that is just the start of our pursuit of our persona and other potential psychological pitfalls. Becoming 'complete' is becoming exhausting in this epidemic of ego-enhancing, obsessive behaviour. Sigmund Freud had a point when he only promised his patients that he would turn their 'neurotic misery' into 'ordinary human unhappiness'. The pursuit of happiness – the belief that superlative, untouchable, sustainable, happiness is possible – is a psychological odyssey without end.

This is not in any way to denigrate the important place of therapy with trained therapists, in confidential contexts, dealing respectfully with real and relevant issues in people's emotional lives. This work is serious. It is not trivial. But it is sometimes confused with and diminished by salacious Jerry Springer-type television exposure, unethical intrusion and public consumption of the vulnerabilities of others that pose as therapy.

Casting a critical eye, then, on this public confessional trend, by which the untrained in psychotherapy expose the susceptible to dubious, momentary mass media celebrity, is a valid challenge to the big buck business of self-help hyperbole.

So it is perhaps appropriate and timely to ask why we are preoccupied with the unobtainable? Is it time to ask where we are searching, why we are searching, what we are seeking, from whom, with what consequences and when we will know that we have found what we are looking for?

Perhaps it is also opportune to ask why we would dismiss from consideration, if only at a purely pragmatic level, the research that shows the physiological and psychological advantage and assurance that having a religious belief contains for those who have it.

Research on the relationship between religion and health includes findings of better health behaviour and increased life expectancy, with lower rates of death from cirrhosis of the liver and from emphysema. It shows increased resistance to addiction, including alcohol addiction in adolescents. Religious belief brings about immune system improvement, pre-surgery calm, shorter hospital stays, quicker recovery from depression and enhanced bereavement healing. It provides routine, increased social support and social participation.

And religious belief enhances not just health practices, but creativity, artistic endeavour, literary imagination and scientific pursuit. From Albert Einstein's affirmation of the relevance of the Divine and Abraham Maslow's hierarchy of needs, the pinnacle of which is the therapeutic power of the transcendent, to the seminal work of such thinkers as Carl Jung, Gordon Allport, Michael Argyle and Viktor Frankl, there are many works affirming the relevance of religion in our lives.

Alfred Adler approached psychology on the assumption that 'the soul is part of life', in contrast to many mechanistic psychology models. Biofeedback studies affirm the therapeutic power of prayer in that there is a measurable physiological response that accompanies it. Harry Aponte examines a spiritually sensitive psychotherapy, while writers such as Donald Bardill emphasise a traditionally Christian approach. In light of this, there is an extraordinary contradiction, then, between the preoccupation with health and the dismissal of religion, given the benefits of the latter upon the former.

Recent societal analyses have also demonstrated the inverse relationship between happiness and prosperity. They suggest that economic restoration may have caused a reduction in social capital. Or to put it another way, the more we have, the meaner we are; the more we have, the more miserable we are; the more miserable we are, the more we want. This is a social conundrum and societal challenge.

The question is this: is what we seek more easily and freely available through religion? Is it more gently and generously given, more altruistic in its aspirations, more inclusive in its invitation, more meaningful in its message and less transitory in its transcendent horizons? All religions have something to offer. But maybe, for example, a religion that has at its core the command 'that you have love, one for another', and all that such love entails in real enactment, is not a bad social model, psychosocial system and psychological intervention for our times.

After all, religion may have got there first with 'the good life'. Ironic when you consider the fortune we spend on detox, deprivational therapy and gratification delay, essential oils and incense burning, uplifting incantations and musicology, nutritional guides, individual and group therapy, autogenic training and meditation.

Do fasting, Lent, Benediction, church choirs, fish on Friday, Confession, Sacraments and the power of prayer sound similar to you? Intriguing!

POSTCOLONIAL
ANARCHY

The fear of being dominated and dictated to runs deep in the human psyche, deeper still in any colonised country; fathoms deep in our Irish psyche, with some still flinching at the memory of colonial oppression. Indeed, the psychological consequences of occupation can take many lifetimes to erase.

Colonisation is not just possession, it is dispossession: raid of land, rape of pride, suppression of language, subjugation of religion and slavery of body. It is educational deprivation, starvation and famine, and the deeper starvation of the cultural core, distorted and disfigured by the relegation of a population to the sidelines of itself.

Colonisation cuts to the heart, corrodes the soul and erases cultural identity. That is why it is challenged so exceptionally, why it is remembered so vividly and revenged so ruthlessly. When colonisation ends, freedom rarely begins, because of the psychological and sociological damage that inevitably ensues.

Recovery can take decades and is protracted if any party perceives that there is injustice, inequality or unfinished business in how the relationship is terminated and in relation to who gets what and who keeps what when 'independence' is finally achieved.

Like a messy divorce, achieving 'independence' in this country led to divided loyalties, fights over who went with whom, who wanted what, who had a say in it, who did not, how it was negotiated, how it was settled, who felt cheated, who felt coerced and who gained.

There were the national custody arrangements in a 'family' where some wanted no change, some wanted to join the departing party and others wanted to remain behind. Inevitably, some on both sides simply got stuck with the one they did not want.

But the further tragedy of the aftermath of 'occupation' is that when independence is finally achieved, a series of even more oppressive regimes may be self-imposed. This is because in any postcolonial society what becomes most important to it is usually that which it was previously most deprived of. This frequently brings about an over-correction, an extreme swing in the opposite direction which propels a people too far from the centre in an attempt to get as far away as possible from every reminder of a past oppressive regime.

Ironically, in the attempt to recoup the pre-colonial past, eradicate all traces of occupation (consider the destruction here of many Georgian buildings) and regain a denied era, foreign oppression may be replaced by a different domination. In Ireland, in the attempt to restore our lost language, revive local customs and reinstate religious practice, another ascendancy ensued: one that has met its own demise in recent decades with a further swing too far from centre in the opposite direction again.

The psychological oscillations in the aftermath of occupation and recuperation may include the triad of hurt, fear and anger and a postcolonial, post-traumatic, anti-authority anxiety, suspiciousness and hyper-vigilance for any imposition, demand, control or constraint upon the person, his or her possessions, place, practices or philosophy.

This may explain many of our current practices as a people, particularly our ambivalence with regard to law.

When a legitimate authority replaces an occupying authority, the habits of generations in circumventing the controls of the coloniser may continue in a new, irrational and damaging form. There is, perhaps, a kind of atavistic national memory, which says that to adhere to the law is to collude with the enemy, to party with the oppressor and thereby betray and inform on your kin. Colonisation takes its toll on a society; postcolonial freedom does not begin when the coloniser leaves – there is a postcolonial legacy to be dealt with.

But what is the legacy of this, our past, and what psychological consequences, if any, has it had on the individual in this society? One possibility is that it has contributed to the propensity of many people to flout the law, equate authority with autocracy, view obligations as impositions and see organisations as systems to be outsmarted.

It is this that may have allowed a generation to drink and drive, to avoid due debts, to kill for land, to segregate, to castigate and to dominate anyone who posed a real or imagined threat to absolute freedom. It is this that may have caused a generation of individuals to hoard money and to secrete surplus earnings from benefiting its own people. This may explain the cartel-based collusion and corrupt institutional cheating of which we have now become embarrassingly aware.

The undercover mentality, the resistance, the covert activities to outwit, to outsmart, to circumvent and to operate within the loopholes rather than the spirit of the law, within what can be got away with rather than the ethics of living, and to regard all institutions and enforcers as 'suspect' – that is one postcolonial legacy. Perhaps the tribunals to resolve the outcome of that mentality are testament to how endemic that mindset has been. The hope lies in our young adults, our post-postcolonial young European generation not burdened by the ambivalences of the past.

There are other questions concerning our national psyche that we might ask ourselves. For example, is it the legacy of fear that makes us feel threatened by others of different culture, see immigration as invasion, asylum as imposition and equate foreign with foe? Or is it just singing too many ballads over too many pints that conjoined foreign and foe in mind and memory?

Is it simply that we were once poor and are afraid of being poor again, or that we were once downtrodden and are afraid of being oppressed again?

Is it fear of religious imposition that makes us evade ethical considerations? Is it fear of deprivation that causes us to be afraid that others will take away from us what we have so recently retrieved?

Or is this postcolonial story just a story, a narrative of injustice and blame to explain the less worthy of our actions as a society?

If the past is so precious, why do we destroy it? Why do we bulldoze our archaeological treasures, commercialise our most beautiful resources, tolerate with pitiful penalties illegal dumping, permit noise pollution unimaginable in other capital cities? Why do we profit from sale of shoreline, mountain and lake and privatise what should be available for everyone?

We have a paradoxical relationship with the past – a hostile attachment whereby we simultaneously revere, idealise, vilify and demonise it. We have a bizarre relationship with wealth and poverty, with high tolerance for the visibility of each. We have a world record for generosity towards people in other countries – provided that they remain there and do not dilute our homogeneity of race, creed and culture.

Yet we have youth who have wholeheartedly embraced what it is to be European; global ambassadors abroad demonstrating the quintessential vitality, intelligence, compassion, creativity and humour which have been an equal hallmark of our diverse and devastatingly engaging Irishness.

It is time to think about who we are and what we wish to become. Time to resolve the paradoxical absurdity between reverence and demonisation of the past. Time not to 'look back in anger', but instead to look ahead. Freedom is not gained through an event: it is a process and a state of mind. It takes time, and we have had time, to adjust, to exorcise the past and to exercise the benefits of freedom.

Societal analysis may be outside the direct province of psychologists, and there are many sociologists, historians, philosophers, anthropologists and archaeologists who can inform the present with the discourses, details and demographics about who and what we were in the past and how that may or may not have contributed to who and what we are today.

John B. Keane, our much-loved master of storytelling, put it thus: 'We are the tenants of this millennium and we are the tenants of these years behind us.' In the first decade of this millennium, which is still new, perhaps it is time to let go of past oppressive narratives and co-construct new, magnificent, imaginative and magical narratives for a better, more ethical, more sympathetic, more just and more aesthetic future.

If we were to do so, what new inclusive tenancy could we create?

LOSS
AND
SUFFERING

Introduction

'What will survive of us is love' wrote poet Philip Larkin. To live is to love; to love is eventually to lose or be lost to another. To lose is to suffer and grieve the loss. To grieve is to encounter that most quintessential human emotion of mourning for that which has gone, when, in the words of Emily Dickinson, 'everything that ticked has stopped'.

Love and grief are inextricably bound. One cannot grieve if one cannot love. It is the ultimate demonstration of our humanity. It reveals the heart and exposes the soul. It is life at its most raw and most real. It is the universal unifying force between people: our fundamental vulnerability, our essential frailty, our exceptional strength and the extraordinary capacity to go on by those who 'have longed for death in the darkness and risen alive out of hell'.

Sometimes loss takes the form of neglect: the absence of acceptance, of care, of being valued and nurtured. Children who are not loved shrivel in size, in body and soul with the anaclitic depression of despair, while couples who struggle with infertility are deprived of babies on whom to gift their love.

Words must be few about the death of a child, respectful, sparse, pared down, as in poet Seamus Heaney's 'four foot coffin, a foot for every year' encapsulating the grim geometry of young death and the measure of its immensity.

Against the insult of grief we are both struck down and ennobled. Love that is lost brings sadness and regrets, personal anniversaries and private pain: 'the sudden piercing loneliness, like a knife'. Yet if it is painful to lose someone else, to lose oneself must be incalculable, as in 'the long goodbye' of Alzheimer's and the consequent erasure of one's memory of oneself.

And grief is something that children often learn about with that first loss of that special family friend, the companion of childhood, the family pet. Sometimes loss and suffering take the form of loneliness before the solace of solitude is learned.

Living, irrespective of the time in which one lives, inevitably brings the experience of loss and the suffering that loss engenders. The articles in this section explore the emotions that we encounter when confronted by the many losses described above and the psychological manner in which we attempt to make sense of loss and of ourselves in these human encounters and transcendental happenings.

Infertility:
Living without
Children

With so much focus on the trials and tribulations of parenting, it is easy to forget that there are many couples who would give anything to have their own children. These are the one in six Irish couples who spend years battling with infertility and with infertility treatment, many of whom at some point have to learn to live without their own children in their lives.

Couples without children suffer an invisible grief that runs too deep to share with those who may never have considered the possibility of childlessness. Like many of our most profound human experiences, insight into the sadness of childlessness is often only gained through personal pain.

Couples for whom contraception and limiting their fertility is the issue simply cannot comprehend the terror that seizes those who cannot conceive, or who cannot carry a baby to full term. It is an insidious suffering because it is over an extensive period of time that people realise that they are being refused access to parenthood and all the attendant stages that being a parent involves.

Infertility spans a range of psychological issues in its relationship to bereavement, loss, mourning, isolation and social exclusion. Like bereavement, it is a process with many stages. The first stage is the realisation that pregnancy is not the automatic event it was anticipated that it would be, with the alarm this realisation brings. What was assumed is not routine, is not available. It is being denied.

Couples who encounter infertility often encounter the classic 'any news yet' queries so beloved of families to newlyweds in the aftermath of marriage. Enduring these insensitive euphemisms is described as one of the most annoying early aspects of childlessness. Much worse are the rather crass aspersions cast on sexual prowess, as if sexuality and fertility are the same. Some men describe receiving the most humiliating innuendos from other males, as if impotence lies at the heart of the problem, while successful women have been accused of choosing career advancement above motherhood when they have not produced offspring in the time perceived to be acceptable by observers of their childless state.

A second stage of suffering occurs when the friends of couples without children begin to have children. There is grief for women visiting girlfriends in hospital with their new babies. It is additionally painful for women without children to have to accept the unavailability of their friends as they get caught up in their new, baby-focused lives, often with new friends and friendships which they have developed with other mothers through meeting them at crèches or playschools and other child-centred activities.

Even when couples retain their friendships with couples who have children, social occasions can be dominated by discussion of children, thereby excluding them from the 'club' of parenthood. Women feel this exclusion as if from a 'secret society': the sacred shared experience of pregnancy and motherhood. Men suffer equally on the sidelines and feel sorry for their wives in these situations, knowing how conversations dominated by children can be upsetting for them.

But many couples say that the medical intervention stage is the worst. During this distressing and undignified period, private life, personal relationships and physical body are invaded, followed by the roller coaster of hope and hopes dashed. Artificial constraints on the relationship may turn intimacy into an expensive, timed technique within which love can be lost in the quest for conception. Worse, in times past, medical visits often found women in waiting rooms with pregnant women or mothers with new babies attending their postnatal check-ups.

But the sadness men and women feel is often for each other. Men are acutely conscious of what motherhood means to a woman. Women grieve the deprivation of fatherhood suffered by men. Inevitably one partner feels 'at fault' and reassurance by the other does little to allay that sense of not having given to each other an entitlement that it seems to be so easy for other couples to achieve and even impossible for some to avoid.

Some couples therefore describe feeling extraordinary anger toward young single mothers and fathers who seem to them to conceive so carelessly, and treat so flippantly, what they, as a couple, struggle to achieve. Some find themselves locked in avoidance of all reminders of what they cannot have: advertisements on television featuring children, children's shops and toy stores, schools at playtime and meeting their friends when their children are at home. There are couples who are amazed at how angry they feel to be amongst the percentage of people who will not experience parenthood first hand. There are other couples who find that they emerge well from the process, that they embrace their coupledom and come to appreciate their alternative roles as significant people in the childhood lives of their extended families and friends.

And in the final stage of the infertility journey, as couples recognise that they may never have their own biological children, the issue of adoption may emerge. Too exhausted for yet another long-haul emotional process intruding into their married lives, it may become too late to be a parent.

Some couples differ about adoption, which can divide them at an already vulnerable time. Others agree it is not for them. Still others experience joyful adoptive parenting and discover that parenthood is less about biology and more about the reciprocity of love in cherishing and rearing another human life.

But for those who continue to be childless, new courage is often required to adapt to life without children: a task rendered difficult because of the plethora of annual societal events around parenthood, the most poignant being Mother's Day, Father's Day and Christmas.

Those who are part of large families encounter child-centred celebrations – nieces' and nephews' birthdays, religious ceremonies, exams, debs, graduations – the litany of events in extended family life. They are also often victims of the erroneous belief that couples without children have endless time to assist family and ageing parents and should take on more responsibility than their siblings with children.

The childless 'only child' may be relieved of the extended family occasions but may exchange this plethora of events for other losses. It is sad to be the last man or woman in a family line. The extent of this loss will depend on the culture, the nature of the family business or the importance of the family name, but almost all people in this position experience some form of guilt with regard to the ancestral line.

Infertility is a specific couples experience. But for some couples without children, motherhood may have been both given and denied, thereby complicating the emotions of sadness and guilt beyond belief. One partner, for example, may be tortured by the memory of a past baby 'surrendered' for adoption about whom their spouse is unaware. There are women who had an abortion during their teenage years, at a time when having a child seemed to be the worst thing that could happen to them, who find themselves in the paradoxical situation whereby not being able to have a child seems to be the worst thing that can happen to them now. These are extraordinarily complex emotions.

There are women who have survived cancer, whose saved embryos did not survive or for whom implantation was unsuccessful and there are women who suffered stillbirth or miscarriages to the point of being unable to go through that terrible loss one more time.

For couples without children the future holds practical worries about which partner may die first and how the other partner will survive that loss. And amidst grief for the potential child of whom they have been deprived – that idealised, that imagined, that possible yet impossible child – there may be acute sadness that there is no such child to inherit one's wealth or to tend one's grave and to keep one's memory alive.

Womanhood is not confined to motherhood, nor is manhood defined by begetting. Yet couples without children are often special in the knowledge they hold about how sacred the capacity for giving life is. Frequently they present a model of marriage, of love and togetherness that is unique because of their shared journey, the persistence of their mutual support and their amazing kindness to other people.

Few reading these words will not have, amongst their friends, at least one such couple, who gave from a well of love, denied expression in parenting, support to other people from that source. And many childhoods have been graced by the memory of the fun, generosity and the presence of those couples who had attention to give to other people when nobody else seemed to care.

With the exquisite irony and interweave of life, these couples without children often 'have' many children who owe a large part of their success, their feelings of worth, their career choices or their confidence to the interest, influence and guidance provided by them.

DEATH OF
A CHILD

———————

It is hard to write about the death of a child. It is something too sacred. To describe is to diminish. Words do not suffice.

Those who have suffered the death of their child need no depiction from others who have no right to describe their world. Only they have that right. They have passed through the darkest night of the soul and a child's death is beyond human words.

It is hard to write about the death of a child for those who have not experienced it. Who would want, even momentarily, to imagine that event? Better not to. Fate should not be tempted by thoughts. Better to hope, as all parents do, that it will never happen to them.

But it does happen. When it does there are a thousand angers. Why me? Why us? Why my child? What purpose under heaven could such suffering have? Why go on when you outlive the child who should outlive you? What life is this that could allow this death? Grief is exhausting. Grief is active; a brain in pain with memories and images, eidetic of remembrance, remembrance of moments that made up a short life cut short.

It is no wonder we are afraid to think about the death of a child, or that research has found it to be the most protracted, the most painful and the most difficult grief to encounter. And while the acute stage may eventually fade, parents who have lost a child describe a special kind of sadness that lasts forever. Each family and extended family member is affected in his or her own way. Grief is unique to the person who grieves.

There is no childhood stage and no parent age that is easier than another to lose a child. No child is acceptable to lose. It may be eldest, youngest, only son or daughter, one of many children or an only child. It may be a miscarriage, stillbirth, neonatal death, 'sudden infant death', childhood illness or injury, an accident in adolescence, a car crash, the tragedy of suicide or the horror of murder.

When a child dies, how the death occurred, why it happened, if it was inescapable or preventable, the circumstances surrounding it, if there was time to prepare or no forewarning, are all factors that affect the grieving process.

Grief is especially complicated when death is sudden, particularly if there were any prior angry parent–child exchanges to torture parents with the thought that this was their last conversation with their child. They forget that everyday parenting often involves demands and commands. Adolescence inevitably contains some days of discontent. It is unfathomably hard if death occurs on that day. Parents in that situation need to remind themselves that it is only those whom we love that we bother to admonish. It is in the context of care that parents censure. Their children know this.

Regardless of how or why a child dies, guilt is the conventional companion of grief. Witnessing an ill child evokes a sense of helplessness in parents. Anticipatory grief may allow some preparation, or perhaps it just removes the element of the unexpected and its associated shock, yet even when what is foreseen occurs it is not really expected, for the young should not die and their death cannot be accepted. The process of living through the dying of a child takes much courage.

There is an added dimension to grief when a child dies, as with the passage of time that child's friends grow up and achieve the lifecycle stages denied the dead child. Watching their dead child's pals become teenagers, or teenagers become adults, parents find themselves trying to imagine what their own child would have been like at these stages. What would their child have enjoyed, what talents would have unfolded, what personality would have emerged, what family resemblances would have appeared, what career choices would have been made, what life would their child have had, had life not been taken away?

Guilt is dominant in the sad situation of suicide because families feel that there must have been something they did that contributed to the despair, or something they did not do to alleviate it that they should have done. Unimaginable is the agony of discovery. Grief is interwoven with trauma, anger and the crippling belief that what the person was feeling and planning should have been noticed, could have been stopped.

Suicide brings apprehension about what to tell, to whom, how and when. How private or public should the funeral be? Suicide brings the ignominy of an inquest, that sadness of hearing the details of death, a sense of stigma that life was concluded this way.

Research reveals a child's murder to be the most extreme, excruciating and long-lasting sorrow for parents, for this is a sorrow that lasts forever: the sharper edges may in time be dulled, but the dulling of life from the day the death is discovered is without end. No child's death is acceptable, but death that was preventable is never acceptable. Anger and outrage abound. There is autopsy, inquest, arrest or no arrest, and what has been described as the criminal 'injustice' of a system that many parents perceive to be more protective of perpetrators than of their dead child. No sentence meted out to the murderer of their child can ever be as long as the life sentence their dead child received when life was taken away.

And overriding all grief is the difficulty for couples, each of whom may be too pained to help the other; or both parents too overwhelmed by grief to help their other children; whole families enveloped by mourning in a world where life outside grief has ceased. Grief is physical, heavy, immobilising and blindingly difficult to see beyond.

It is hard to know how to help families who lose a child. But if we do not learn to help those who mourn, we may hurt them by our absence or blunder into their grief.

Because parents of a dead child want no empty words: no clichés, no assurances about time healing or death having a meaning in the greater scheme of things. No reminders that burdens are not more than backs can bear. No statements that one 'knows' how they feel: only those who have lost a child can know that and even they can only know their own loss, for the end of each life is a different defeat. Parents do not want to be told that they have 'angels in heaven' but to hold in arms that ache, the child of their lives, here and now, safe and close, on this earth with them.

ALZHEIMER'S

Alzheimer's is a progressive, degenerative, neurological disorder causing deterioration in crucial cognitive capacities. It is distinguished by depletion in memory and language, disorientation in time and place, misplacing belongings and potential eventual corrosion of competence in everyday familiar physical and self-care tasks. Alzheimer's arises from nerve cell destruction or abnormal protein in the brain: the so-called 'plaques' and 'tangles' microscopically visible and metaphorically descriptive of the entanglement of the mind.

Its triggers are many. Risk increases with age. Family patterns suggest a genetic component. The condition may also be found in some people who have Down's Syndrome, with reported increased risk in their siblings. Additionally there are suggested environmental activators, such as head injury. There are proposed environmental averters such as the consumption of oily fish or omega 3 fatty acids, while cerebral callisthenics and other mental workouts are recommended to maintain nimbleness of mind.

In Ireland there are almost 40,000 people with dementia, Alzheimer's being the most common form. There is no single diagnostic test: its early signs may have a multitude of explanations. Memory tests and brain scans assist diagnosis, as does excluding other potential causes of dementia such as vascular dementia, Lewey-Body, frontotemporal lobe dementia (including Pick's disease), Parkinson's and alcohol-related dementia (Korsakoff's Syndrome).

Alzheimer's progresses in stages over a number of years, each stage heralding new challenges and requiring increased personal care. But much can be done to delay Alzheimer's course: medication to assist anxiety, memory and retention of new information and practical strategies to divert difficulties, while early diagnosis allows time for important life-adjustment and design. Families need time to organise short-term and long-term support, time for consideration and decision on available treatment options to maintain capacities as long as possible and time to make financial and legal arrangements that may be necessary later.

From a psychological perspective, Alzheimer's contains all that we fear most. What makes it so frightening is its capacity to change irretrievably the person you love. It is the ultimate threat: annihilation of mind, obliteration of memory, alteration of personality and destruction of life itself. It is loss upon loss, death before death, life rewound, memory erased and cognition confused. It is the fusion of past and future into a permanent present of receding recollections. It is a long goodbye to life.

Alzheimer's may begin in mild forgetfulness: the elusive word on the tip of the tongue, evading naming. It may involve the repeated story, the thrice-told joke, the forgotten request, the lost belongings and the frustration of disremembered phone numbers. Sometimes it is the disappearance of a question while asking it, evasion of an explanation while providing it, of a story in the midst of telling it, or re-reading the pages of a book, seeking their sense and being confused by their complexity. It is arrival at the top of the stairs without recollection of what object was desired when that ascent began, finding the hairdryer in the fridge and the butter in the bedroom, as the thoughts and objects of life hide, confuse and diffuse themselves in a world where one becomes increasingly befuddled, bemused, baffled and bewildered by the exigencies of life.

This is what makes the onset of Alzheimer's so difficult, because it may mimic the memory loss of other conditions, including stress, work overload, the side effects of drugs, infection or depression. It is an enemy to be feared because it is an enemy in disguise, camouflaging itself in common forgetfulness. With Alzheimer's there is no sharp swipe of the grim reaper's scythe but an invisible stalker, lurking in the intellect, picking its way through the crevices of consciousness, attacking critical faculties, dismantling communication, confusing comprehension and reaping what remains of people's remembrance of the events of their lives.

What is it like to observe someone you have loved all your life slowly metamorphose into another, identity sabotaged in this insidious way? Only those who have lived this reality know. There are many thousands of people who have encountered this enemy: prisoners of war returning, they know the shape of its territory, the strategies for survival, they have unmasked its face, heard its voice, learned its language and identified its weakness. They have sourced their own amazing strengths in dealing with this invader. Their bravery is unquestionable, but what is so surprising are many who say that Alzheimer's was more manageable than they initially imagined.

Amidst the burden of care – and let us not ever idealise or minimise the unremitting, unsupported burden that can be – are also special moments of humour, of closeness and of compassion in the role reversal in which the child parents the parent and the parent depends on the child. They say that there are times of extraordinary shared laughter when an object appears in an unlikely place, a sentence is distorted, people are called by other people's names, reality is inverted and families participate in this surreal reality, in this parallel 'behind the looking glass' world. Like Alice in Wonderland, where words seem to mean 'whatever you want them to mean', where 'things get curiouser and curiouser'; where people grow and diminish in a second, where identity is diffuse, where nothing is as it seems, where characters hop in and out of existence and where the only predictable is unpredictability, families who care for someone with Alzheimer's share an experience that is uniquely theirs.

These families say that identity is not lost; the opposite happens. It is critically examined, conserved, narrated, celebrated and protected by those who love the person with Alzheimer's in their determination not to allow this alien invader to erase the soul. Like nations who guard the essence of their culture at the threat of invasion, families guard the identity of the person whom Alzheimer's afflicts with a distinctive, creative determination, so that what is being erased by the disease is being simultaneously inscribed in the annals of others' memories to forever 'remember those who cannot'.

LONELINESS

AND

SOLITUDE

Loneliness is a universal experience. It is painful in the extreme. It lies at the core of most mental health conditions. It is one of the emotions primarily associated with depression and accompanies most suicidal ideation and intent. While its aetiology is complex, its prevalence is clear, as it reaches epidemic proportions in society today. There are many very lonely people out there.

It is said that loneliness is articulated least, but may be experienced most profoundly, by men and that suicide is often an expression of deep emptiness that is as physically distressing as it is mentally exhausting. While women experience loneliness, they also seek, and often find, immediate alleviation of its most acute aspects by talking to each other about their feelings. Men tend to express emotion differently and one of the crucial mistakes we make might be to ask or expect them to express their feelings in the same manner as women. If this is not their way, then their own way is both dismissed and denied.

Christmas is, of course, a high-risk time for loneliness, with New Year a time for contemplation of who we are, what we have achieved and how we hope to go forward into the year ahead. This may uncover a core of loneliness that is kept at bay at other times.

Episodes of loneliness can range from isolated incidents to acute attacks. Loneliness is the inevitable companion to bereavement and an integral feature of grief. This is why mourning begins when we realise the extent of the loneliness that lies ahead in the void created by the loss of someone or something that we love.

Most major psychiatric distress is distinguished by the loneliness endured by the sufferer: the isolating fear of the perceived ill will of others in paranoia, the experience of estrangement from reality in psychosis, the loneliness of obsessive-compulsive repetitive rituals that other people are not burdened by and the loneliness of delusional belief: holding perspectives and experiences not shared by other people, thereby having one's own reality invalidated.

Phobic fears cause exclusion from activities enjoyed by other people: for some, the ultimate loneliness of agoraphobia and social phobia is that it severs contact between the sufferer and the wider world, making every foray outside the home an agony of terror and every social expectation an excruciating embarrassment.

For some people, the experience of loneliness is triggered in situations that are similar to the first episode of it, the very first time when the event and the emotions accompanying it occurred. For example, the childhood experience of being sent away from home may produce acute homesickness in a person when faced with any subsequent separations later in life. For others, chronic loneliness forms a melancholic backdrop to their lives: a predictable pattern of pessimism, dejection and wretchedness which people try to hide.

Some people are acutely lonely during specific life-cycle transitions. Adolescence is one such stage. Consider the lonely musings of Adrian Mole, his dissatisfaction with his physical development, his propensity to be misunderstood by other people and his unrequited adolescent passion for Pandora.

Adulthood without a partner may also bring profound loneliness, portrayed in countless Irish works of fiction. Who could remain impassive before the quiet desperation of these lives: Tarry Flynn's cry to the Lord above if he'd ever love or the barren futility expressed in *The Lonely Passion of Judith Hearne.*

More poignant still may be the loneliness *within* relationships, between intimate emotional strangers bound by obligation. Remember the cold moment of realisation by Gabriel Conroy in James Joyce's story of 'The Dead'? Standing at the window near his sleeping wife, watching snow fall 'all over Ireland upon the living and the dead' and knowing that he could never compete with the celibate passion his wife shared with the young Michael Furey in her youth.

Loneliness defies definitive definition, but most descriptions emphasise its negative aspects. It is distinguished by its paradoxical nature: its isolation is felt most profoundly amongst a crowd. It lurks in the existential angst of being thrown into a world of other people. It is assumed in the anomie of alienation, the ennui of societal disenchantment and has been the source of philosophical speculation into the meaning of 'being' and of 'nothingness', concepts through which we may come to understand more about ourselves.

Loneliness lies at the core of human longing, spiritual yearning and the quest for belonging. Our fear of loneliness is not actually fear of being alone, but the fear that nobody wants to be with us. This negative definition of loneliness prevents us from enjoying the psychological enrichment that being alone can bring.

Ironically, solitude is something many of us unashamedly crave. It is the acceptable face of 'loneliness'. It understands the joy of being by oneself, the aesthetics of being alone: the opportunity for insight from 'sessions of sweet silent thought' through which self-discovery may emerge. If we did not try to combat loneliness, we would not experience the many toxic antidotes that invade our lives.

With iatrogenic irony, the more we attempt to fill the emotional space occupied by loneliness, the more we fill its silence with sound, its solitude with activity, its emptiness with entertainment, and the desire for companionship with technologically generated soulless company.

Worse still is the profusion of psychobabble, the proliferation of self-help programmes that may send false messages about the nature of psychological health. These suggest that total emotional control, great social success, cognitive competence, strategic organisational skills and psychological perfection are available commodities.

They enjoin us in the words of Bernard Farrell's Dr Fell to 'relax', 'relate', 'communicate'. In supreme psychobabble they invite us to 'name', 'claim' and 'tame' our anger. They try to 'cure' our loneliness. They define us in numbers; they describe us in patterns. But perhaps they miss the point.

And in this lies a question: why are we afraid to be alone? What definition of the human condition have we concocted that makes it unacceptable to enter into and embrace the universal and human experience that loneliness provides? How and why did we come to definitions of psychological health that omitted being alone as an acceptable condition?

Because in the quest for self-understanding, it may be that instead of struggling against the experience of loneliness, we might begin to appreciate it. We might be proud of our capacity to be alone. We might redefine what we mean by 'lonely' in lovely, positive terms.

The word 'alone' is derived from 'all one'. This etymology points to the completion to be found just by being yourself: one person, all one. It says that we are complete if we are prepared to spend time with ourselves without the clamouring need for people to be present. It says that in solitude we discover ourselves: that understanding emerges through silence. It says that you are sufficient. It says you can choose to be you and that has a totality that does not require, although it might desire, an other.

The healer of the self may be the self. We may become 'all one' by being alone. We may anoint our sorrow and remove our pain simply by entering into, rather than avoiding, the experience of the self. Mystics and monks and druids have always known this. Poets and writers and musicians have also always known that creativity is born out of the self, alone. Our most profound moments are often alone.

Secret Anniversaries
of the Heart

Historic anniversaries are public and visible. Each society has its own commemorative dates. Some are cause for celebration. Others are shameful remembrances. There are man-made catastrophes and natural calamities, stories of survival and narratives of fatalities. There are public holidays and parades, plaques to be placed and bouquets to be laid. There are new years to be rung in with fireworks and festivities, old battles to be remembered, dead heroes to be honoured and living legends to be fêted.

On some commemorative days there may still be veterans with personal memories. But with the passage of time, historical annals may define which anniversaries are celebrated and which are not, depending on their significance socially, culturally, scientifically, economically, geographically, politically or in terms of international relationships of war and peace.

Anniversaries remind nations of the momentousness of historical events so that ideally the best human endeavours may be emulated and the worst may never be repeated.

Institutions also mark their progress since their establishment. Professional bodies celebrate their foundation. Educational institutions commemorate their origin, venerate their founders and celebrate advances since their inception. Anniversaries are important psychological stocktaking activities. Often revering the old while initiating the new, they maintain mental continuity between present and past. They mark the passages of time, the progress of humanity and plans for future progression.

But public holidays are only one form of remembrance. There are also private remembrances. These are personal memories. They are private anniversaries that go unmarked, although they may recall the most important occasions in someone's personal life. They are held in the heart while the world continues in its busyness, unaware that this day and date are special to that person and will remain so forever.

The most obvious example is the first anniversary of a death. On such occasions the world does not stop, although it seems as if it should 'stop all the clocks' and pause to remember our personal loss. It continues unaware of the significance of the day. It does not know that this is an anniversary. It is callous in its casualness, cruel in its continuance, cold hearted in its disregard for private pain, refusing to commemorate this day that deserves remembrance. There are many such days in ordinary people's lives. Poet Henry Wadsworth Longfellow describes them best: 'The holiest of all holidays are those, kept by ourselves in silence and apart: the secret anniversaries of the heart.'

Each day, somewhere, someone, keeps a 'secret anniversary of the heart', often holding it close while externally acting as if the day were just another ordinary day. These secret anniversaries can take many forms. They may be joyous: remembering first love, a wedding day, the birth of a child, the achievement of a goal, the realisation of a dream, the publication of a book, the resolution of a problem or some very special successful family event. One may hug to oneself the private precious memory that 'on this day, so many years ago, such and such happened which only those involved remember'.

But sadly, many secret anniversaries are sorrowful: the birthday that nobody recalls, the anniversary of a stillborn child, the death of a young life, the diagnosis of illness, the death of a husband or wife. These secret anniversaries of the heart may also include the tragedy of suicide, the road traffic accident, the time a person went missing, the day a body was found, remembrance of the closing seconds of a parent's life, the rupture of a relationship, collapse of a dream, end of a marriage, the injury that disabled, the phone call, the ring on the doorbell, the seconds that changed the remainder of life.

What courage does it take to live a private anniversary, a secret anniversary of the heart, inwardly grieving, outwardly functioning, pretending that this day is like any calendar day?

People display this courage every day. There are people doing so today. The tragedies that make up daily news have anniversaries that those involved must face each year and for all those years, long after the newspaper reader, the radio listener and the TV viewer have forgotten the specific terrible event.

But it is not just the newsworthy that is worthy of mention. Life brings loss. Loss brings anniversaries of the loss. Families face memories of family members, of those who have died, of those whom they miss. Anniversaries awaken emotions. They remind one of the intensity of relationships that are not erased by the passage of time: that years do not obliterate memory although they may soften the acuity of pain. They show that one is capable of survival, even when life deals its worst. They provide the opportunity to reaffirm existence, the continuity of connection with people we have loved.

Anniversaries of the heart show that each of us is called to live out 'our one, our own and only life' in the best way that we can, remembering the past, facing the future, while embracing the memories of those who shared our living with us.

Longfellow had it right. These tender memories, these secret anniversaries of the heart, need no public proclamation. They are precious in their privacy, sacred by their silence and kept by us for others, as in time they will be kept, perhaps, by others for us.

Losing a
Special Friend

When a family pet dies, a family member dies. Families grieve in a way that is incomprehensible to those not reared with or owners of pets. Outsiders observing the depth of family grief often think it inappropriate, given the tragedy of human loss. This is beyond dispute. Respect for the dignity of human life is supreme.

But the loss of a pet, of that little life, that dependent, vulnerable, all-loving life, is a loss nonetheless of amazing proportions. And it touches us in a unique way each time it occurs over a lifetime of living with, loving and losing pets. Grief is not measurable, quantifiable, competitive or comparative. Nor is love. No pattern guides us, no warning deters us, no logic, no reason, no rational sense steers these emotions. No preparation for death shields us. And the loss of an animal is acute because animals love us unconditionally and, in turn, teach us the power of unconditional love.

Animals are not impressed by achievements or educational qualifications, celebrity, accent, acquisitions or accomplishments, social connections or political power. Animals are not influenced by appearance, status, dress or wealth, accommodation or address. Kindness, sensitivity, being allowed to live in proximity to humans, under human protection, is all many pets require. A simple shelter, a safe place, enough to eat, the joy of affirmation and interaction, and considerate intervention when injured or ill: these basic necessities of living suffice for the purity of spirit of animal life.

Love of animals is not the province of the sad and lonely, though animals may counteract both emotions in all of us. Love of animals is not compensation for the unattached, because animals play unique roles in families large and small. Love of animals is not a counterbalance to social exclusion, though human acceptance rarely matches the unconditional acceptance by animals of their owners. Nor is loving animals the last recourse of the defeated, though when the chips are down, animals will never let you down. Devotion to pets is not the province of 'elders', though the security, protection and companionship animals can provide in later years, as well as in early life, is enormous. As for the tired stereotype of the spinster with her cats, that belongs to an era as moronically out of sync with the reality of people's lives as gender jokes and racial jibes.

Loving animals is a privilege, a gift bestowed upon us, often by parents, whose own parents bequeathed that special understanding of the significance of animals in nurturing the young, developing sensitivity, teaching responsibility, appreciation of nature and communication at levels that are deeper than words.

What parent would not welcome a child minder who loved their children unconditionally, welcomed them home each day deliriously, befriended them continuously, guarded them diligently, protected them viciously, consoled them in misery and joined them in play? The family with a dog has all those things and the well-cared-for animal is a source of love and learning for a child. The ostracised child has an adoring companion. The excluded child is not alone. Having an animal facilitates friendship making amongst children or consoles the child who has no other friends.

The child with disability learns that love is not dependent on ability. And in a world where others may seem more proficient, a child's sense of capability is enhanced by guiding a baby creature through the mysteries of the world.

From an animal a child learns patience: it takes time to build the trust of fragile things. Children learn to respond, not on their own whim, but on the need of another living thing. Wishes must be delayed while an animal is attended to, provided with water, groomed and walked. The animal's need for exercise ensures activity for the child: an important consideration with recent child obesity concerns.

But it is the therapeutic power of animals that is the most impressive: their reassurance, silence and capacity to 'listen' with rapt attention to a child's woe. Empathic when the world seems hostile, animals support children emotionally and immeasurably. They provide what children need most, a reliable loving presence that simply stays by their side.

That is why we grieve so profoundly when a pet dies, companion to childhood, a primary attachment and the first encounter for many children with the finality of death when parents are still present to support their child through the intricacies of grief and recovery.

Love and grief are intimately and bizarrely bound. If one is unable to love, one is unable to grieve. Grief often brings us into the better part of ourselves, unites us in the stark rawness of our human capacity for attachment, for love and for mourning when the source of love and attachment is no more.

Animals in our lives teach us many things and at the end of their lives they teach us how to cope with loss and how we can recover yet continue to love and remember the best friend of childhood forever.

Vicarious
Traumatisation

Is it possible to be traumatised by exposure to someone else's trauma? Could you, in some extraordinary vicarious way, experience the shell shock of war, that 'carnage incomparable', as if you yourself were on the battlefield? Could your ears hear the 'stuttering rifles rapid rattle' and your eyes witness the grim, grotesque grimaces of death? The answer is yes: secondary exposure to trauma brings susceptibility to sharing some of the suffering and psychic pain of the traumatised, a condition known as vicarious traumatisation.

This new landscape of psychological susceptibility is particularly significant in a world that has recently experienced relentless ravages of terror, atrocity and geopolitical gloom. We inhabit this world. We are all vicarious voyeuristic victims, technological intruders and consumers of the minutiae of misery all over the world on our screens, in our ears, in the immediacy of this information age. And it is making us miserable, excavating our atavism, increasing our pessimism and shaking sacred certainties in the concept of civilisation. As a result, many of us are suffering from vicarious traumatisation.

Vicarious traumatisation is the cumulative impact of repeated exposure to secondary traumatic material. Research in this area has shown that the recipients of traumatic narratives, secondary witnesses of traumatic events, may develop many of the signs and symptoms of post-traumatic stress disorder (PTSD) or prolonged duress stress disorder, particularly if they form an enduring empathic engagement with the traumatised. These PTSD signs include vivid flashbacks and re-experiences of the event, distressing dreams, physical reactions, feelings of detachment and estrangement from others and hypervigilance which entails suspiciously scanning the world for signs of danger, each sign a flashback signal of potential threat.

Which of us cannot recall 9/11 in forensic detail like some 'consensual hallucination' or fictitious filmic fragment replayed again and again, both by media and in our minds? What 'memories' do we retain even of times before our time: the concentration camps, the naked emaciated living dead, shrivelled faces pressed against wire fences, children with old men's eyes staring, faces frozen, in flickering black and white cinematic clips? Were we not there? We were. We share the transgenerational transmission of that trauma.

Amongst those who are 'there' daily and who are particularly susceptible to vicarious traumatisation are mental health workers at the coal face of human suffering. These are the people who work in the terrible terrain of sexual abuse, rape and violence; those who work with refugees, the homeless, the dispossessed, the tortured, the imprisoned or people demented by injustice, deranged by drugs, overwhelmed by grief or betrayed in childhood, at the mercy of their memories, rewound and replayed in an eidetic effluent of horror. Researchers Laurie Anne Pearlman and Karen Saakvitne suggest that therapists may empathically experience a parallel trauma influencing multiple aspects of their personal and professional lives. Vicarious traumatisation may induce anxious and avoidant behaviour, feelings of anger, of cynicism and sadness, compassion fatigue, psychic numbing, emotional anaesthesia and a sense of isolation from family, friends and colleagues.

Of course, the notion of potential occupational trauma is not new. In the 1970s, Herbert Freudenberger's concept of 'burnout' identified the physical and emotional depletion that can result when workers chronically experience critical incidents and traumatic events with subsequent psychological aftershock. Service providers are particularly predisposed: brave peace guardians like our Garda Síochána, fire brigades, ambulance crews, mountain rescue teams, lifeboat service, coroner service, indeed our entire *seirbhísí rialtais* and the men and women in A&E who repair the ravages of living, dignify dying and deliver our dead. While this work is not new, the context is new and the scale is stunning; summed up in the familiar figures of our state pathologists carrying their bags to the latest disfigured, dismembered cadaver casualties of crime.

What is also new is the choice of vicarious violent occupations for our children: video visions of viciousness on a scale we would never permit them to view in 'real' life, games dependent on the ability to annihilate an arbitrary enemy, expertise in the 'entertainment' of killing, 'where death becomes absurd and life absurder'. Surely, we cannot continue these vicarious cruelties and desensitise the young, or to paraphrase poet and soldier Wilfred Owen, cauterise their senses so that with hearts 'small-drawn' they can 'laugh among the dying unconcerned'.

Through vicarious traumatisation the map of our psychological world, our cognitive schemata, has been disturbed, reshaped and redrawn as surely as the map of the world now contains unfamiliar spaces and places. We have acquired a new war nomenclature that says the opposite of what it means, a disembodied vocabulary that hides the reality of what it names in surgical strikes, collateral damage, smart bombs and friendly fire. This bizarre semantic sanitising of reality desensitises us to the actuality of conflict. We are caught in verbal and emotional polarities: material wealth versus spiritual bankruptcy, evil acts against the axis of evil, innocence and guilt, liberation and occupation, war on terror and the terror of war, dictatorship versus democracy, democracy versus dignity. We straddle the political polemics of war and peace, East and West, North and South, while the refugees of recent wars stream into our cities to uncertain welcome, racist revulsion, compassionate care or extreme exploitation.

Psychological understanding of the emotional milieu of war began with recognition in World War I of war neurosis and shell shock. Vietnam veterans introduced us to PTSD. The accumulated impact of subsequent local, national and international conflicts, allied to our media exposure and engagement with intimate strangers on all sides of conflictual divides, now conscripts us into vicarious traumatisation with combatants in an 'eternal reciprocity of tears'. This is our apocalypse, now.

Don't You
Walk Away
from Me

———————

Don't you walk away from me. With those angry words chasing her, a young fourteen-year-old girl walking with her cousin and her dog in a park, in daylight, near a playground for children was set upon by a group of equally young girls.

The story goes that two girls held the cousin back while the leader of the gang and her pals set upon her and beat her until interrupted in this deadly delight by a passer-by. An opportunity for escape from an unprovoked, unwarranted, incomprehensible attack.

Why should this event capture the concern of the nation in a way that similar events happening to young boys daily do not? And why have we become so complacent about the ritual, regular beating up of young boys by other young boys that we now leave it unmentioned, unaddressed and unexplored? Why are we so desensitised to violent behaviour that we are not clamouring for reasons and solutions? What makes violence the new sport of young women? Where is this anger coming from and where will it end?

There are many explanations provided for this new violence amongst women. Some suggest that girls have been given an ambivalent message that 'anything boys can do you can do better' and that this has translated into 'I can drink as much, become as drunk and fight my corner as well as you'. The role models are confused and the only models remaining for girls are aggressive models.

Some say that women have become so objectified, so used and abused in how they are sexualised and portrayed in ads and in magazines, that they receive no respect and that they have no respect for themselves or anyone else.

There are many who believe that new family configurations and changes of partners, parents and living place have produced a generation that is parented so sporadically and sparsely that they are running riot. There are no boundaries, no rules and nobody to enforce them. What can young people do when nobody tells them what they cannot do?

Of course, there are those who blame parents who work, that they give too much, that this is a generation that is deprived of nothing except their parents' time. They say that they wait for nothing, look forward to nothing and do not know how to tolerate a moment of frustration or an instant of denial.

There are significant numbers of mental health professionals who have seen the effects of media violence on the behaviour of young people and the part it has played in acceptance of images of cruelty. This is a world where attack is without consequences, without reality, without any understanding that this is a real person, not a target or reward on a film screen or a computer game. Indeed, many are sickened by the graphic, gratuitous violence that is the visual world of the young.

Finally, no debate would be complete without discussing the

influence of alcohol and how it releases and unleashes the impetuous, disinhibited anger of youth who are bored, neglected and frequently blind drunk.

On radio recently we listened to a mother tell the story of her daughter's trauma. We listened to her shock that there was no apparent motive for the assault. We heard her question how she, or any mother, any parent, could keep their children safe. We heard some explanations, sociological, psychological, judicial and official. And we heard that startling phrase by the attacker – 'don't you walk away from me' – that began the most violent episode.

Because we *have* walked away from this generation. Despite all our analyses of them, we have not analysed ourselves. We have not provided them with places to go, role models to aspire to and stories to inspire them. They have little to look forward to and we have not created enough of the structures, boundaries, predictability, consistency, compassion and control that young living creatures need to grow. We are not a society that is seen to be in control of ourselves, our drinking, our spending, our pricing, our fighting – our own behaviour. We look for more and more external controls to make us behave – speed traps to catch us speeding, laws to stop us littering, penalties to stop pollution, racial regulations to reduce our prejudices, and elaborate corporate, institutional and financial systems to stop us robbing each other blind.

Violence is learned and we have taught them well. We have not taught them to control their behaviour because we do not control our own. We cannot give them what we have not got ourselves.

And in the cry of a young girl for attention and the hurt of another young victim of violence lay the plea of a generation:

Don't you walk away from me.

How we answer that plea is our challenge, not theirs.

GRIEVING
VALENTINE

'All my life's bliss from thy dear life was given
All my life's bliss is in the grave with thee.'

Emily Brontë

Valentine's Day. Celebration of Love. Pictures of Cupid flying above. Valentine's Day. Your loss more immense. Heartache increased. Pain more intense. Valentine's Day. Remembering you. There's no place for singles when everyone's two.

For many people, Valentine's Day is yet another of those annual events when consciousness of being alone in a world of couples is heightened. Psychological research shows that the confluence of commercial forces, societal norms and personal pressure to participate in St Valentine's Day all contribute to stress surrounding the Westernised celebration of the day.

This is not surprising. Valentine's Day is the day when romantic love is privileged. Therefore, all those whose relationships have ended, who have broken up with boyfriends or girlfriends, who are single, who are separated, divorced or bereaved, feel the singularity of their situation on this day. It is a busy day for the Samaritans because the depths of loneliness, of difference, of exclusion, of feeling unloved, unwanted and unattached, are confronted by many on Valentine's Day.

Valentine's Day is a day when the death of a spouse, particularly if the death has taken place in the past year, is felt even more acutely. An aching loneliness lies in knowing that there is nobody from whom a Valentine's card with loving messages will be received. It is a time when the display of cards, 'Happy Valentine to My Loving Wife' or 'Valentine's Wishes to My Darling Husband', are excruciating reminders of a world of loving that has ended. It is a time when the finality, the lived reality of the death of the person one loved is once more confronted.

There will be no florist at the door, no surprise present, no mobile message, no restaurant booking, no clink of champagne glasses, no shared bottle of wine, nowhere special to go, no one special to go with, on this day dedicated to togetherness.

There will be memories of past times. Of other Valentine's Days, when being a couple was taken for granted and, like many losses, unappreciated until it ended. There may be guilt, because guilt stalks lovers and mourners, finding the minutiae with which to torture the bereaved, to berate them unfairly, on special days and especially on Valentine's Day.

Guilt finds the moment of carelessness in a lifetime of devotion, the one request refused in the generosity of giving, the minute of anger in a marriage that was a loving partnership. This is why people often have regret at what now seems like neglect, when romance was ridiculed, a gift not given, love not romantically conveyed, when a Valentine's Day in the past was allowed to pass uncelebrated. Guilt forgets that one single day does not define a relationship: that love is not always articulated in conventional ways. Guilt forgets that couples have their own way of celebrating Valentine's Day, some subscribing to its commercialism, its excuse for celebration and romantic expression, while others participate in a perfunctory way.

But when one is alone, celebratory events can take on new meaning. On Valentine's Day, therefore, for those who have lost a partner there may be loneliness, stark and sharp, sadness at the amputation of the future that was planned together but that now must be undertaken alone. There may be envy of others who are unconscious of their privilege, casual in their coupledom, unaware of the awkwardness of being alone on a day that celebrates having a special 'other' in one's life.

For some there will be consciousness that the relationship with the person who died was not perfect, sadness that what might have been was not and now cannot be; that death has denied the hoped for difference; that disappointment is concretised by death.

For others whose marriage seemed perfect, the light of its perfection may overshadow the possibility of ever finding happiness in life again. Or so it may seem on Valentine's Day.

Grief is relentless. It finds ways of reminding, admonishing and ruminating. It is seldom predictable. While universal in pattern, it is personal in its particularity. As poet Emily Dickinson wrote, 'I measure every grief I meet with narrow probing eyes. I wonder if it weighs like mine or has an easier size.' This is because grief is immeasurable, complicated, complex and incomparable. It is our surest sign of our capacity to love.

Grief on Valentine's Day is, paradoxically, the ultimate marker of love. For Cupid's arrow does not just pierce to attract, but to attach. It pierces most deeply those who love most profoundly. Grief for another is the ultimate marker of the love of that other.

It anoints with remembrance. It embraces with regret. It enfolds the person who was loved in loving recollection.

And therefore, while one may be alone on Valentine's Day, that aloneness is a special kind of loving not accessible to those who have not passed through the mire of mourning which is the ultimate expression of love. Those who mourn are blessed, for they know they have the capacity to love.

FAMILY, KINSHIP
AND
RELATIONSHIPS

Introduction

Few organisational structures can compete with the psychological permutations and relationship convolutions of families. There is no emotional terrain more loving, more all encompassing, more supportive, more perfidious, more loyal, more incomprehensible, more straightforward, more maddening and more reassuring than the network of home, family and kinship relationships. Family membership is life membership of a complex, dynamic system. A family is not a static thing. It is a system in progress. It is one that has phases and life-cycle stages through which its members travel together over time.

Consider the nuclear family: parents, children and the intricacy of the relationships amongst them: being the eldest, youngest, middle child, first son, only daughter or 'baby' of the family and the impact on children of the relationship that exists between their parents when they are born.

Families are places where children respond to the arrival of new babies, places where everyone knows but nobody will admit who is closest to mother, to father, to siblings and each other. Everyone knows who is in conflict with parents, which family members perceive themselves to be different, isolated, excluded, ignored, or favoured, affirmed and privileged. Families have unconscious alliances, coalitions, rivalries: dyadic, triadic and dynamic interactions that may shift and change over the years as people alter their understanding of themselves and their relationships with each other.

Children in families often invite, acquire or have identities foisted upon them: black sheep, golden-haired son, the clever, sensible, responsible, successful, creative, challenging one. They may be the hero, the martyr, the rebel, the compliant and the accommodating child. Children always know who occupies what role at any time.

These articles reflect upon some of the relationship roles that arise in families. There is marriage itself to explore; the extraordinary love that women have for their magnificent men; and the intricate, unarticulated intimacy between fathers and sons.

Whole volumes could be written in praise of aunts whose exceptional psychological role in family life has been woefully neglected, while the bond between grandparents and grandchildren unites them in a deeply loving, transgenerational kinship tie. Adoption holds a special place in family life. Families respond in many ways when gay children decide to come out. Of course, seasonal events can bring family feuds, yet everyone needs to call somewhere home. Home is where you are from, families are where you belong, which is why the sale of the family home can cause such amazing angst.

MEN ARE
MAGNIFICENT

Men are magnificent. They grace the lives of women with their presence, their perspective, their protection and their love. They give to those they love the security of their attendance, the balance of their perception, the humour of their viewpoint, the audacity of their conviction, the strength of their bodies, the benefit of their skills, the angle of their intellect, the exhilaration of their individuality and the pure male energy that emanates from men.

To the ears of women, few sounds can compete with the hearty laugh of men, few comic sketches with the quirkiness of male imagination, few decisions with the vigour of male verdict, few poems with the sparse words with which men speak about their lives. Few images can compete with the heartrending sight of male tears, male grief and loneliness.

Yet few injustices can compete with the current ever-increasing injustice in the negative construction of men, of masculinity and of manhood. It is time to challenge these descriptions of masculinity as a homogeneous and unchanging category. It is time to celebrate men.

Deficit-defined masculinity, like media-defined femininity, diminishes men and women, sets them in competitive combat and reduces to a gender war their social roles, their heartfelt concerns, their cognitive distinctions, their emotional expressions, their justifiable anger, their personal interactions, their complementary cohesion and their love for each other. It diminishes them in how they speak about each other. Like the fictional *The Female Man*, it defines relationships as antagonistic rather than as a shared challenge.

That challenge is how to be men and women together in the world today. The question is not what terrible traits lurk in men or in women, but what expectations do men and women have of themselves and of each other? What social roles do they embrace or discard? What shared goals and aspirations, what injustices to each other and to themselves do they identify and defy and what unity lies in their fears?

Postmodern psychology increasingly understands that 'trait views' of intrinsic individual differences must expand to recognition of the interactions between gender, class, race, society and the cultural context in which men and women live. The days of dichotomies are over. Relativity, uncertainty principle, chaos theory and postmodernism have ended the era of absolute truths. But they have not yet rescued men from negative gendered attributions any more than they have liberated women from the structural inequalities that shadow their lives.

Men have been analysed and 'therapised', constructed, deconstructed, neutralised, desensitised, sensitised and, particularly, personally and harshly criticised. They bear the brunt of blame for patriarchal privilege. They carry ascriptions as abusers, rapists, plunderers, warmongers and perpetrators of violence.

The boy becoming a man finds himself the object of fear and

of suspicion to women as he walks home alone. He is the subject of derision if he chooses macho male interpretations of manhood and the object of contempt if he opts for alternative definitions of being a man. He struggles with an oversimplified stagnant stereotype within which violence by males is portrayed as normative masculinity, as predator and terminator with poor impulse control, inadequate anger management, limited expressive language and restrictive emotional literacy.

Market forces, in the interests of selling their services, portray men as domestically inept, socially untutored, emotionally moronic, globally irresponsible, irrepressibly corrupt and personally exploitative. These are outrageous definitions of the men whom women love. Because while most violence that is perpetrated may statistically be male, most men are never violent. Violence is not an inevitable trait lurking in men. It is a transgenerational behaviour that is first learned and later chosen by some people. It is not easily eradicated because of the societal unwillingness to name it, to acknowledge it, to address it and to provide alternative role models for those young men who are most at risk of perpetuating it. The task for men and women together, however, is to investigate the contexts in which violence occurs, to protect each other from violence in whatever form it occurs and not to level gender accusations at each other.

Clinical experience reveals that few people are as strong as a strong woman or as gentle as a gentle man: that many men are as willing and as able as anyone else to enter into respectful facilitated psychotherapeutic discussion about the dilemmas in their lives. Men are neither afraid to feel nor feel afraid to express their feelings. They are not victims of the 'despotism of fact'. They do listen. They do talk. They do love. They do care. They are hurt. They show extraordinary compassion when confronted with human distress. They form attachments. They will ask directions. They can be romantic. They read more than maps, they are *not* from Mars: they are of this earth, which many have farmed, tended, respected and resourced.

Men have worked for, worked with and loved women since the dawn of time and it is time to appreciate them. Many enrich the lives of women with their special humanity, their extraordinary vitality, their unique physique, their physical strength, their modern heroism, their incomparable compassion, their unparalleled gentleness, their masculine energy and their exuberant love.

They are our sons, our brothers, our uncles, our nephews, our grandfathers, our fathers, our husbands, our companions and our friends. 'Men' as a category must not be abstracted from the men we know. They are much loved by women and it is time to tell them so.

FATHERS
AND SONS

Fatherhood is special. The relationship between fathers and sons is special. It is a unique connection of exquisite gruff intricacy. It is central to emotional development and mental health. It is a significant factor in the development of the baby, the exploration of the infant, the courage of the child, the strivings of the adolescent and the success of the adult. It may make and shape a young man's attitudes, values and beliefs. It is one factor which determines his tolerance or prejudice, his behaviour towards women, his expression of aggression, his views of marriage, of divorce, of love, of sex roles, of self-esteem. It is one key in his capacity for compassion and his acceptance of the splendour of manhood in its most honourable manifestations.

The father–son relationship is the exclusive domain of men. It has sometimes been privileged, often derided, occasionally obsessed about and frequently fought about in ridiculous, unnecessary and illogical competitive disputes about the influence of motherhood versus fatherhood on the child. This is because fatherhood, like motherhood, is a socially constructed role. In the past it confined itself almost exclusively to patriarch, protector, provider, decider and disciplinarian encapsulated in the catch-cry of many childhoods: 'wait till your father gets home'. It disparaged men who wished to child-care with caricatures of apron-bedecked pram pushers, equally deriding the role of women at that time. It denied many men their capacity to nurture and know their children. If, tragically, parents lost a child, a father grieved silently, as if this dead child was not *his* child, swallowing the exclusion of the question to him of 'how is your wife coping?'

When their own fathers died, denied the chance to show the craggy compassionate care that many men express wordlessly to each other, sons also grieved silently; grieved for what might have been, for time not spent together and for words that were said or not said to each other, for memories of the texture of a coat, the fixing of a toy or the tallness of paternal protection. Indeed, sons whose fathers die young or who leave, neglect or reject them in childhood move into high-risk categories for later adolescent and adult depression unless the loss is acknowledged and addressed. For it takes a man to teach a boy about the best that manhood can be and it takes a role model to show a boy how to be a parent.

Fatherhood also has a unique impact on men. It is not just mothers' hormonal levels that change with childbirth. Fathers' testosterone levels plunge by as much as one-third when the new baby comes home. This conflicts with the many images in Irish literature of the absent, ineffectual, feckless, avoidant and violent father.

In sport, men march on the football pitch with miniature versions of themselves. In word and song, father is father, da, the old man, papa and pa and of course 'my dad'. What boy does not love to hear himself described as 'son', and there is no greater joy in a young child's life than spending special time exclusively with dad, doing what 'men do', striding out together or making, mending, creating, fishing, walking, talking or not talking and bringing out the best in each other simply by being together.

Psychodynamically, Sigmund Freud's famous 'Oedipus complex' represents sons as incestuously inclined, envious, in anxious competition with their fathers for their mother's love. This was beautifully expressed by Frank O'Connor, whose short story on the subject resolved it better, perhaps, than Freud, by father and son colluding as comrades in adversity when the new baby arrived to replace them both in 'mother's' affection. And who could ignore Adrian Mole's description of his father's definition of the 'perfect son', plunging the boy into adolescent angst at the impossibility of being what his father wanted him to be? For no son ever wants to disappoint his father. No father wants to hurt his son. Yet often neither is sure how to achieve what they want to be in each other's lives.

So how do fathers determine what their sons will be? The accumulated research evidence of three decades confirms that fathers who are warm, supportive and involved can assist the cognitive, academic, social and emotional well-being of their sons. Self-concept, stability, conduct, school behaviour and substance use are amongst the factors researched. Rejection by fathers has been associated with adolescent delinquency, polydrug abuse and most especially with dissatisfaction with life and high levels of depression. Rejection generates frustration, anger and emptiness and young men show most anger when they are most hurt.

Boys usually imitate their fathers. Good and bad, they imitate them. If fathers are not there, whom can they imitate? Many boys from fatherless homes have been found to be less well adjusted, less competent in forming friendships and frequently confuse masculinity with violence, achievement with power, sexuality with aggression and sex with coercion.

Conduct problems often mask the yearning of a son for his father's attention and approval. Sons usually love and admire their fathers more than their fathers may know. Fathers usually love and admire their sons more than their sons may know. Clinicians who work with families frequently observe, from professional sidelines, the ache for attention and acceptance between fathers and their sons that gets diverted into anger and hurt, destruction or depression and disappointment in each other. Women therapists watching this process must also acknowledge that we do not know what it is like to be a boy or man, a father or son, but that it is of immense dimension in relationship terms. It is the most significant male-to-male relationship. It has little to do with 'begetting' and everything to do with commitment; it is a lifelong venture, it unfolds in everyday communications and conversations. It is made.

So what kind of relationship have you made with your son? How much time do you spend with him? What things do you do together? How does he know that you love him? How does he know what you expect of him? What qualities do you admire in him? What is the nicest thing you ever said to him? What, if anything, is the worst? What does he admire most in you? What behaviour does he copy? What, if anything, does he wish was different in your relationship? What kind of man will your boy be and what will he remember most about you when you are gone?

What do you think he would answer if he was asked those questions?

The father–son dyad is as intimate as a scrum, as triumphant as a try and as celebratory as a conversion when fathers and sons are in warm relationships with each other. But it cannot succeed without time, training, tactics and commitment. When the opportunity is lost, the 'match' is lost. This is a cruel defeat. Time spent, not money spent, is what sons remember. Fathers too need recognition for what poet Robert Hayden calls 'love's austere and lonely offices' so that their sons will not regret, as the poem 'Those Winter Sundays' regrets: that 'no one ever thanked him'.

Father's Day:
What Kind of
Father Are You?

Every day is Father's Day in many Irish families. Fathers are on to a winner. They enter the condition of parenthood without morning nausea, nightly cramps, nine months of progressive bodily enlargement and the process of giving birth. Research shows that marriage and fatherhood are good for men. They are the least likely to suffer depression. Single men and married women suffer depression far more often and mothers are twice as likely as fathers to suffer, particularly mothers with three or more young children.

Research on fathers is extensive. It shows that fathers usually hold the power, the purse-strings and the physical strength. Fathers are the givers, or withholders, of money to their wives, of maintenance to their ex-wives and of pocket money to their children. They are often less impoverished after divorce than the rest of the family.

Fathers decide on and purchase the family car. In two-car families the father's car is usually larger and better, although the mother's car is used for the transport of children, school runs, dental and medical visits and grocery shopping. Fathers attend school functions less frequently. They are less likely to attend fairs, plays and gym displays, parent–teacher meetings and sports days. Fathers are less likely to attend with children for medical, psychological, dental, orthodontal and other appointments.

Irish surveys show that over two-thirds of children would talk to their mothers if worried about 'anything'. Three times as many children would talk to their mothers than would talk to their fathers if they were worried about things at home. More children talk to their mothers than to their fathers if they are worried about friends, or if they are being bullied at school. As many as 81 per cent would seek their mother's, rather than their father's, advice if they were worried about issues of health.

In families where both parents work outside the home, the main responsibility for child care and housework still falls on the mother. She is the one who does the laundry, who scrubs the bathroom and who takes time off work if children are unwell. It is fathers who often go for a 'pint' after work while mothers collect children from childminders and prepare the family meal. Fathers sometimes help with household tasks, but do not yet consider these to be their responsibility. Fathers, however, decide on the family holiday, they make the major household purchases, particularly for entertainment such as stereo, TV and PC. Research even shows that during family TV viewing, fathers hold the remote control.

Hands up: how many fathers can honestly say that they have spent enough time with their children? How many fathers parent by remote control? How many of you know what power and importance you hold in the lives, the happiness, the development, the security and future psychological well-being of your children?

You are the creators of memories, the providers, the guardians of childhood, the role models. You have the capacity to be gentle, sensitive, nurturing, caring. You are the person your small son wants to be like when he grows up. You are the one he emulates. You are the map which guides him now and into the future. You are the father your daughter is proud of. You are the person she feels cherished, guided and protected by. You are the one she shows off to her friends. You shape her belief in herself and her trust and belief in others. You are the powerful, magnificent, omnipotent, all-knowing and all-solving figure in the lives and imaginations of young children. You provide self-esteem to the child and the teenager, you let them know if they are worthwhile or worthless.

The betrayal of such power, such potential, such possibility, is both sad and tragic. Betrayal of children takes the form of disinterest, indifference, neglect, physical abuse, harsh and unjust punishment, violence and the ultimate betrayal of sexual abuse. Betrayal occurs when money needed for children is squandered, gambled, drunk or withheld. Betrayal occurs when children witness or receive violence. Betrayal occurs when children are disappointed, let down, disregarded, neglected or rejected.

Betrayal occurs when fathers absent themselves from their children's lives. With tens of thousands of Irish marriages having ended, are there fathers who do not spend Father's Day with their children? Who could not feel sad for the seven-year-old girl whose parents separated when she was a child, and whose father maintained poor, irregular, unpunctual and disappointing contact with her? Like many children whose parents separate, she secretly believed that she was at fault, and even more secretly imagined that she could help her parents to re-unite. Her hope ended on Father's Day. For weeks beforehand she had designed, coloured, painted, crayoned and painstakingly prepared a Father's Day card. It held the simple message 'Daddy I love you'. He left it behind, forgot it, just as she felt he had left her behind and forgotten her.

What of the fourteen-year-old boy who yearned, pined and mourned the loss of his father, who had left home for another relationship? He sent him a Father's Day card to remind his dad that he was a father. And how many adolescents are brought to psychologists to 'cure' them, when all that is required is paternal time, attention, affirmation and love?

The accumulated evidence confirms the importance of fathers in the lives of children. Strong attachments develop between the baby, the young child and the father. The differences in interactions (for example, mothers hold babies to caretake, fathers to play) enriches social development. Many boys from fatherless homes have been found to be less well adjusted, less competent in forming friendships, more confused about sexual identity, more confused about masculinity (often equating aggression with masculinity) and more likely to be 'delinquent'.

It has been found that the highest proportion of adolescent 'delinquent boys' come from fatherless homes. Disruptive behaviour at school is often an attempt to gain paternal attention. Conduct problems often mask the depression felt by boys who feel rejected by their fathers. The famous work of J.B. Wallerstein and J.S. Kelly on the effects of divorce shows the pain, yearning, anger, grief and severe disruption experienced by children and adolescents and their wish to retain contact with their fathers. The loss of a father in childhood is one of the greatest risk factors for depression in later life. Research shows how often boys who lose their fathers suffer depression, while adolescent girls experience upset and distress and often have difficulty in opposite-sex relationships.

Father's Day is celebrated once a year. It is the day to thank, acknowledge and admire those many fathers who are all that a child could wish for; the day to forgive fathers who have found parenting difficult; the day to ask their forgiveness for not inviting them enough to be part of their children's lives, for not showing them the important, gentle, caring, nurturing role they play. For not reminding them that they are central to the happiness, security, self-esteem, safety and physical and psychological development of their children.

In Recognition
of Aunts

―――――――――

One of the benefits of being part of a large family is that your children are conferred with immediate membership of the extended clan. The nature of the clan is to care for its own. The ancestral ties, the sequence of succession and the strong connection of kith and kin surround the newborn with a relational chain of familial concern.

There are cousins with whom to be close or competitive. There are grandparents to adore and be cherished by. There are uncles and aunts, facsimiles of parents or engagingly different in age, appearance and perspective. This wonderful network of connections is provided to advance and augment a child's perception of the world.

From this important family network, one much neglected relationship is a child's lifelong attachment to a favourite aunt, particularly an aunt who has retained the so-called single state. This role is insufficiently attended to by psychotherapy, yet it is one of serious significance to the developing child. Inimitable, irreplaceable, inspirational, the place of the aunt on the family genogram deserves much greater attention than it currently achieves.

From the child's point of view, the unattached sister of its mother or father brings, to the clutter of family connections, a perspective on life that is not available from other family members preoccupied with rearing their own children. The single aunt, as family member, contributes enormously to family life, playing a role of unique importance in the world of a child by her emotional availability and distinctive love for all her nieces and nephews.

And while the bond between a child and married aunts, mothers of cousins, may often be strong, for many there is exciting exclusivity about being 'the special child', or if really lucky, the godchild, of the so-called 'maiden' aunt.

Indeed, a surprising number of adults still recall with the primitive jealousy of childhood their dismay when single aunts married and produced 'their own'. Despite all the reassurances, deep in their hearts they knew that abdication of their own unique emotional space was inevitable with the arrival of infant dethroners. They grieved the loss of being special and especially loved and no longer being their aunt's 'child'.

In the past, many children experienced their first train journey and first introduction to city life or rural life by having a holiday with their aunt. For a child sent alone to stay with her, she was the person who would provide the treats and the experience of being, if only for a precious few days, away from siblings, with the attendant joy of being the object of total attention.

Others, whose aunts lived nearby, had the reassurance of her proximity to the family home, the sweet security of her as babysitter, her support for their own parents and her presence in times of crisis, which often relieved children of inappropriate adult burdens when family life was fraught. Frequently, there was her financial assistance in times of hardship, her arrival if there was a family emergency, her support through family loss, her interest when children were lonely and her role as safe source of venting, disclosure, advice or asylum for adolescents out of favour at home. Part of the family, while apart from the family, the aunt occupied the ideal psychological position to assist everyone in the extended clan.

In the past, when universities were few and were confined to the major Irish cities, aunts came to the rescue with accommodation and support. Today, there are numerous college graduates who might never have been able to avail of university education had it not been for the generosity of their aunts in providing a home for them in Dublin, Cork or Galway, feeding them, minding them, keeping an eye on them, encouraging them in their studies and ensuring that they were supplied with all that they needed to achieve success in their exams and in later life.

Aunts often dedicated their own lives to elderly grandparents, taking upon themselves the obligations and responsibilities of the rest of the family and modelling the role of carer for the next generation. Alternatively, many provided the first representation of self-sufficient womanhood, validating career aspirations and independent living and showing that women could make choices in how they lived their lives.

Around many aunts lay rumours of loves lost, an aura of mystery and romance, gleaned by children through whispered adult stories of past passions, tragic romances, heart-rending endings that could never succumb to mundane marriage and ordinary life.

Meanwhile, those mysterious cloistered aunts who were nuns guarded the family with a mantle of prayer as petitioners for exams, recovery from illness, job success, suitable husbands for their nieces or virtuous wives for their nephews while other aunts were feisty liberation theologians in foreign lands, thereby demonstrating a different dedication of life for others.

In a more conservative and penny-pinching era, young aunts were magical, liberated goddesses who knew the art of extravagance, the joy of living, had wardrobes of clothes, time to indulge in make-up, to use expensive perfume, collect *objets d'art*, buy non-essentials and treat a child to a shop-bought cake and a meal that was not made at home. They knew how to bring a child to the cinema, to the pantomime, to the theatre or to places that parents could not always afford. Their Christmas gifts were special. They never arrived to a house without sweets and treats at the bottom of their bags. They cared about children and children knew they cared about them.

Different, although equally endearing, were the aunts who were teachers, who provided the secret grinds that made school bearable and helped those students who aspired to the seminary, to permanent positions in the civil service or the bank or who even thought of following in their own aunts' footsteps and going to teacher-training college themselves some day.

Aunts had time to share books and money to buy them, gifting a child with a love of books, of reading, of learning and awakened educational aspirations that struggling parents often had no energy to entertain. Sociological records may not recognise the significance of this influence in the educational development of this nation, but colloquial history does. Ask any adult if there was an 'influential' aunt in the family, and most people will immediately recall their affection and gratitude towards one particular aunt who enriched their childhood in immeasurable ways.

Even the older, more stern variety of aunt, those feigners of formality, guardians of etiquette and good behaviour, concealed a revealing twitch to the lip that a child could discern and behind which lay a layer of love that only an aunt could provide. Did not David Copperfield flee to such an aunt, the formidable Betsey

Trotwood, and receive lifelong benevolent benefaction from that eccentric, loving woman? What of Graham Greene's account of his *Travels with My Aunt* or the aunts that peopled the life and fiction of Louisa May Alcott, she herself being a significant maiden aunt? Who could forget the complex interweave in the tale of *Charley's Aunt* or P.G. Wodehouse's depiction of Bertie Wooster's significant if radically different relationship with his two aunts, Aunt Agatha and Aunt Dahlia? Most of all, would James Joyce's short story collection *Dubliners* have been quite so exquisite without those wonderful aunts Aunt Kate and Aunt Julia, without their niece Mary Jane and their beloved nephew Gabriel in that final story, 'The Dead'?

Literature is replete with aunts and while it has too often stereotyped the 'maiden' aunt, failing to paint her deep dimensionality, it has at least recognised how grossly undermined and unrewarded she has been.

Clinical accounts of the role of aunts have alerted psychotherapists to the mental health significance of this role. Free of the demands of direct parenting, many aunts have championed the vulnerable, the bright or the least-favoured child, have seen behind outward adolescent arrogance to the deep sensitivity of a young person's heart, have stepped in to mother on incapacity or death of a mother and have saved more childhood lives than they may ever know.

It is to be hoped that when their own time of need arises, nieces and nephews will remember with equally unselfish deeds the unconditional debt owed to such aunts.

GRANDPARENTS AND
GRANDCHILDREN:
A SPECIAL BOND

The emotional world of the child centres on a few crucial close attachments. One of the most significant of these attachments is that of a child to its grandparents. This is a relationship of immeasurable psychological importance in a child's life, conferring emotional, social, cultural and cognitive benefits on grandchildren.

The grandchild–grandparent relationship is a relationship of transgenerational kinship. It is a declaration of connection, a certificate of continuity and most importantly, a strong bond of love. Indeed, there seems to be a special and unique love that children reserve for their grandparents. This is different to their love for their parents. It is different to their relationship with their siblings, unlike relationships with authority figures and dissimilar to connections with their peers. Yet it may influence the child in most of his or her other relationships throughout childhood and adolescence for those children lucky enough to have the company of their grandparents, at least during their formative years. Some are even luckier and their grandparents continue to be present well into their adult lives and may even be an influence on their great-grandchildren.

For grandparents, the birth of a grandchild is a major event. It is a new life whose origin can be traced back through their own lives with each other, as husband and wife, father and mother, now grandfather and grandmother; punctuating the important life-cycle stages through which they have successfully passed together regardless of other life achievements or disappointments. The grandchild is a declaration of their continuity, their creativity, their gifts, their talents and the essence of who they are, encapsulated and miniaturised in this life, their child's child. It is a trans-generational arc from the past to the present into the future and beyond. It is a bond across time that validates the past and confirms the future. Whatever else has been achieved, the next generation has been brought forth and the generation after that and so the continuity of lineage and life is now assured.

Many grandparents admit that they can enjoy time with their grandchildren that they were unable to savour when rearing their own children. Then the relentless responsibilities of parenting, the daily drudge of work and money, of school and homework, house and home, denied them the time to appreciate their young.

And there are whole generations of grandfathers who, when they were fathers, were banished to the margins of their children's lives in provider roles. These men, as grandfathers, are now seizing and retrieving that 'lost' time to experience the profundity of the company of children and the depth of their own caring capacities. They are giving what they could not give before and enjoying this second chance in the company of children with all the benefits and few of the hassles they recall from their first time round. For grandparenting is also one of the best of roles with children, 'lovely to see them and lovely to see them go', the rear-guard of responsibility rather than the front lines.

And sometimes, through these grandchildren, and through the grandparent–grandchild relationship, grandparents get to heal previous rifts with their own children who have, in the interim, achieved new understanding of life by virtue of becoming parents themselves. Misunderstanding can be resolved, severed relationships restored and another chance is given to all.

Some children are privileged with the presence of both their parents' parents when they are growing up. With advances in medicine and technology and consequent extended life spans, there are fewer children left with the duo of widowed 'grannies' as they usually were in former times. Then, grandfathers were often dead before their grandchildren were born and while grand-children enjoyed time with their grannies, they also felt the absence or the mysterious shadows of their 'forefathers' in the narrative of their lives.

For each grandparent plays a specific role in the child's mind. The assignment of distinguishing descriptions – granddad and granny, papa and nana – to differentiate between maternal and paternal grandparents is more than conversational convenience; it allows a special connection and a particular appreciation of each. In so doing it also often gives children insight into the factors that shaped their own parents' constructions of the world, why they are as they are, why they act as they do and what they might have been like as children.

While the stereotype of shawl-clad, spectacled, fireside, rocking-chair grandmother and walking-stick, pipe-smoking, tweed-jacketed grandfather may no longer be available to the child of today, children often nostalgically idealise 'way back then', 'when you were young', 'long ago' and savour the 'past', the 'olden times' that they imagine their grandparents inhabited when they were young.

This is because grandparents are the holders of history, providing privileged access to the grandchild into the childhood of his or her own parents. They remember what not even a child's parents remember, when their parents were babies, what they were like as children, the things they did, what they said, who they played with, the games they played, whether they were 'good' or 'bold' and whether or not they were temperamentally the same then as they are today.

Grandparents hold the ancestral key in their stories about their own grandparents, thereby allowing children to truly visit the distant past; while the grandson, named after his grandfather, becomes the guardian of the family name, and the granddaughter named after her grandmother knows that she holds a special family place.

There is mutuality in the knowledge exchanges between grandparent and grandchild. They teach each other new things that each needs to know. Children trade the secrets of modern technology for the traditions of the past. They may instruct their grandparents on the Internet, cyberspace, blogging, Bluetooth, mobile text or the finer functions of operating the DVD player in exchange for glimpses into a way of life fast fading, if not already out of sight. Children often share activities with grandparents; complicated time-consuming jigsaws, card games or chess, the skills of being still and listening to silence that are not part of their usual occupational repertoires. They are given the opportunity to 'be' in a different way to the busyness of other aspects of their lives.

Adolescents glow in the acceptance of grandparents. Even the most recalcitrant buckles before the gentle, unconditional regard of an adoring grandmother or the stolid, sensitive solidity of a grandfather's careful comment. Grandparents may be privy to the most compassionate characteristics of their grandchildren, to their caring natures, the softness and vulnerability that may be hidden from parental eyes. Grandparents may validate the struggling child, favour the least-favoured; provide refuge at difficult times, offer stability during parental divorce and mediate between the adolescent and the world. They have advice, communicated in a way that adolescents are prepared to listen to. They are wise.

Grandfathers may provide granddaughters with heart-warming experiences of gentlemanly courtesy, of being treated like 'young ladies', being spoken to with quaint respect and given a sense of value in their gender. Grandfathers also may provide their grandsons with models of behaviour, modes of address and examples of gentlemanly behaviour that is otherwise absent in the current coarse, crude world that children often have to inhabit. The research is clear: children learn from their grandparents merely by being in their presence.

Children who grow up without time spent with their grand-parents sense at a deep, unarticulated, level that they have lost out on an irreplaceable relationship, and the tragedy of parental separ-ation and divorce often includes the exclusion of grandchildren from their grandparents, a special grief for each and a human right denied.

The grandparent–grandchild relationship is an extraordinarily intricate affinity, an exquisite construction by nature to enrich and enhance the lives of both children and their grandparents in incomparable and mutually supportive ways. The model of grandparents is a win-win one. The modern, exuberant grand-parent thinking about climbing Everest shows that the challenges of life are never over, while those who are frail or disabled evoke untold depths of children's compassion which they may carry for the rest of their lives.

And even when a grandparent dies, which is often the child's first encounter with death, grandchildren may understand through their relationships with their grandparents the mysterious seasonality of life, the 'time to be born and the time to die'. And grandchildren may learn, in this way, that people live on after death in the memories that are held about them, and that their grandparents live on because of how they shaped their grandchildren's lives and in the vow their grandchildren make to tell their own children and grandchildren some day about their grandparents, great-grandparents and great-great-grandparents.

MARRIAGE

FIN DE SIÈCLE

Is it possible for a woman to be married and be happy? Well, large numbers of women are demonstrating that it is not. In unprecedented droves, women are packing their bags and, as one woman put it, 'walking back to happiness'.

What on earth has induced women who have been traditionally construed as the cornerstone of the home, the guardians of the young, the containers of self-control, conscience and morality to abandon what was for generations their traditional and supposedly most fulfilling role?

Research on levels of depression says that marital bliss was frequently not as blissful for women as it was painted to be. Indeed, this research identified married women as amongst the least likely people to be happy. Married women suffer depression far more often than their single counterparts. Add three or more young children and inadequate support to the equation and they enter an even higher risk group for human misery.

Conversely, statistics on depression suggest that marriage is good for men, providing them with nurture, status, love, a sexual partner, genetic/biological continuation and a carer of their material world and environment. They have been found to be in better physical health after middle age, to be psychologically less stressed and half as likely to commit suicide as their single counterparts. Indeed, single men have been found to be at significantly greater risk of depression than never-married single women.

But if marriage is supposedly of such psychological and material benefit to men, why are they also moving away so frequently from one marriage to the next? Some suggest that marriage is over. They say that it is *marriages* and relationship diversities, rather than the unique, normative, 'till death us do part', monogamous, heterosexual variety, that are the twenty-first-century, postmodern family configurations. Marriage, as we have known it, is to be replaced by serial monogamy of unpredictable intensity, strength and duration.

The classic explanations for the demise of this most sacred institution have become as simplistic, repetitive and predictable as the classic within-marriage arguments. They have suggested that discontent has centred on who does the shopping, cooks the meals, minds the children, does the laundry and, most importantly, cleans the toilet. In summary, who gets the better deal and who gets the greater street cred for what they do. Having done a cost-benefit analysis, it was found women in particular began opting out.

Traditionally women have complained that their worth has been measured by the menial tasks they undertake, the lack of social affirmation of the housewife or indeed the working wife, the disincentives for women to work outside the home and the prohibitive price of crèche and child-minding facilities when they do. As far back as the 1970s, feminist sociologists and psychologists researching the definitions of men and women in traditional families highlighted that the social construction of marriage and family itself arose from early pioneering paternalistic psychologists writing from the male perspective and the privilege they enjoyed in the nuclear family. Even back then, it was predicted that women would eventually resist forfeiting their name, their independent income and their professional and individual identity to share a secondary vicarious pride in their husband's accomplishments. They would cease to 'look up' to men who were literally above them in age, social status and even physical height. Another explanation as to why people became dissatisfied with their marital roles was that these roles had undergone such a shift.

Today men and women are different, their expectations are different, their self-definitions have changed or been changed for them. The previous apparent complementarity of their prescribed roles with husband as provider and wife as supporter have been transmogrified into a competitive symmetry with each seeking satisfaction, status and support.

Such is the challenge to marriage practices by women that it is reported that a Japanese court in Tokyo ruled in favour of a thirty-three-year-old woman who divorced her husband after he demanded that she do all the cooking, caring, laundry and cleaning in addition to her full-time job.

But if women are re-inventing themselves, men, too, are left in confusion with the ambiguity of their newly prescribed roles. With the dismantling of patriarchal power and privilege, men have been plummeted into a social vacuum from which 'new men' are expected to emerge. They have been analysed, criticised and circumscribed; described in a plethora of popular writings as Peter Pans, Women Haters and Martians, and as being unwilling to grow up, give in and learn how to communicate.

To redress these deficiencies, many men believe that they are being called upon to read and absorb the books which analyse their fears of intimacy and their yearning for it. They object that they are being asked to be emotionally sensitive in the manner defined by women, not in their own masculine manner of self-expression. They are not to be allowed to gain support from the secrecy and succour of previously male-only enclaves: the club, the pub, the snug and the golf club. All kinds of previous crass allowances, in jokes, attitudes and behaviour, have become politically incorrect and legislatively punishable. While attitudinal changes are welcome, there are also many courteous older men who say that they are now afraid to pass the most civil of compliments to a woman, lest it be defined as sexual harassment or innuendo.

The increase in the number of women managers in the workplace allied to the increase in the number of successful female-headed single-parent households has sent a message to men that they are intellectually, biologically and psychologically dispensable to marriage, mating and fatherhood. Many have viewed themselves as dispossessed of all the former symbols of their masculinity.

In the past, a 'good husband' was often defined as a good father and provider with non-drinker and non-violent as added attributes. A woman was defined as a good wife if she was a virgin before marriage, a prolific mother, a careful spender of her husband's hard-earned cash and if she was adequately, but not obsessively, house-proud. Men held the power and the purse strings and the capacity to give or to withhold finance, advantage and protection to their wife and children. They drove the family car, decided on family outings, arranged all the major household appliance purchases and literally and symbolically held the remote control in the household.

Domestic violence was often high and male violence was cited as one of the primary hazards to health in the home, with statistics as high as 20 per cent of wives experiencing it at some time. Many men also claimed the pain of hidden oppression in marriage and research has unveiled a percentage of men who were not just psychologically, but physically, attacked by wives and equally disempowered and disbelieved when they sought legal or social understanding of their situation.

One of the major explanations for the cessation of marriage was that a new social climate and financial support allowed the previously oppressed victims of marriage to leave.

But there is more to it all than this. People are no longer simply seeking the absence of aggression. They are actively searching for multilayered validation of self, gender, role, societal participation and potential. In twenty-first-century dual-career, dual-income families, there is an implicit expectation, particularly amongst equally educated professional couples, that roles are equal, tasks are divided and commitment is mutual. As home help and safe child-minding arrangements become more difficult, expensive and complex to obtain, and as the definitions of marriage and parenthood have become equally more complex, dual careerists are faced with work, traffic and travel, social, financial, emotional and marital overload.

The old notion that children cemented and consolidated a marriage has been replaced by research suggesting that marital quality decreases and stress increases with the arrival of children. Despite the joy and enrichment it may bring to personal and family ideals, the marriage pair now has to negotiate new roles as parents. Furthermore, in the past, even in unhappy marriages, the life spans of marriage, because of the life span itself, was anticipated to be shorter. Now one could conceivably live in wedded disharmony for seventy or more years. What was previously a sacred, procreative and relatively short arrangement has the potential of a life sentence.

Whether any, all or none of the above explanations for the changes in marriage are sufficient, what is significant is that in Ireland there were, at last count, over 120,000 people who had been left or who had left their marriages. This is a cause for concern rather than an object of critique. What is it that has not been provided in our society to allow the continuation and survival of what is indisputably, *when it works,* a valuable, safe, emotional, sexual and psychological context for men and women and a nurturing and supportive milieu for children? I think that we have been too quick to embrace diversity before exploring the possible means of retaining people in relationship, discovering what is required to allow people to live in dignity, mutual respect, equality and love together 'for as long as they both shall live'.

Because marriage is still important to us. And despite the *fin-de-siècle* pessimism and new millennium materialism, the statistics for marriage are doing a turnabout again. While divorce may be rampant, marriage is also on the increase. Marriage is important. It must be so, because the majority still choose it as a way of life at some stage or other.

At the end of the day, despite all the contraindications, there are also clinical and marital therapy findings that many men and women can resuscitate marriages and that they can live together. Up to 96 per cent of the population still wish to do so in their lives. Regardless of the so-called breakdown of marriage, people find themselves wishing and wanting to undertake the process again and again. Marriage has, perhaps, been overly researched in its negativity and further research is suggested into the many happy, nurturing, loving and fulfilling marriages that also continue in this postmodern age. What are their ingredients? What is the crucial factor between workability and unworkability?

Here are some possibilities. In a society that valued marriage, a Constitution that guarded it, a social climate that discouraged divorce and a religious code that was dogmatic in its injunctions that families stay together, there was a belief that relationships were sacred and durable. They were therefore worthy of work during the hard times and understanding during the distressing times.

While one would not wish to return to any form of oppressive past, there has been an overcorrection in our approach to marriage. The media construction of marriage has proliferated an image of erosion, a powerful message of immediacy, consumerism, instant gratification, infidelity and the rights of parents to 'personal' happiness over the rights of children to stability. Media itself has taught us an intolerance of patience, of waiting it out until it gets better. We flick from one channel to the next if subjected to even seconds of boredom. Additionally, many men and women report that they cannot compete with the media images of masculinity and feminism and physical perfection that are portrayed as a norm. If you are not it, you are out.

To have challenged past practices of oppression which at one time were legally sanctioned by marriage was a good thing. But in classic tradition, the baby has been thrown out with the bath water. The best has been lost with the destruction of the worst. Common sense and clinical experience confirm that a good marriage is not a bad way to live one's life.

For the clinical psychologist or family therapist, the pain of marriage breakdown is a daily reality in the eyes of rejected husbands, abandoned wives and distressed children who often feel that they have been forsaken to father-deprived or mother-deprived childhoods or complex shared parenting. Some struggle with confused sibling relationships, with half-brothers and sisters who may be biologically unrelated to each other. Children are often also attempting to deal with a series of parental surrogates. New marriages are increasingly under strain in their attempts to deal with the parenting of these new complex configurations in the reconstituted family. This is not good for mental health, not to mention marriage.

So before we construct too many obstacles to people even imagining that they might love someone through the life-cycle stages into a companionable love and intimacy in older age, let us call a gender ceasefire. Is it possible for men and women to be good friends again? Friedrich Nietzsche may have had a point when he said that 'it is not the lack of love but that lack of friendship that makes unhappy marriages'.

Maybe it is time to stop blaming each other and ourselves for some unfortunate marriages of the past. There were many good ones too. It is possible to re-invent and reconstruct institutions, as we well know from the recent systematic dismantling and renewal of many our most revered Irish institutions. Surely if we have survived what we have survived we can work out new marital roles for a new millennium.

ADOPTION:
PAST AND PRESENT

Relationships are complex. Family relationships are particularly so. The relationships between adopted children and adoptive parents carry extra emotional dimensions that require particular understanding, sensitivity and psychological accommodation. This is because along the convoluted continuum of kinship, assorted family configurations and diverse affectionate affiliations, adoption has held a special and evolving place in family compositions, a place that at times has been misunderstood and insufficiently supported.

Adopters, adoptees and birth parents are intimately linked in a unique triadic relationship chain. When legal adoption was initiated in Ireland in the 1950s during an era when secrecy and subterfuge as a social and familial way of life prevailed, the triad of adopters, adoptees and natural parents contained misplaced links and corrosive disconnections that did a disservice to all parties, despite being instigated to serve the needs of each. Sad that it should have been so when the intent was benevolent: a means of meeting the needs of couples to parent, of children to be parented and of birth mothers to ensure stable, socially acceptable parenting for their particular child.

Unfortunately, the commencement of legal adoption in this country in 1952 coincided with a time of societal silence with regard to sexuality and infertility in addition to the stigma and scandal surrounding non-marital birth. This meant that the 'choice' of adoption was too often an imposition rather than an option for vulnerable women who were ostracised, abandoned and blamed for expecting a child outside wedlock, as if this were a condition they had achieved alone. Additionally, family fears, psychological coercion and societal sanction significantly shaped these events.

In this way, attitudes towards the circumstances surrounding adoption enforced a shameful silence on all involved in the process; mother, child and even adoptive parents, some of whom wished to conceal from others that infertility had denied them their own 'birth' child. This isolated each participant in adoption in their own inevitable curiosity about the other, in their worries about issues of genetic and social identity or, in the case of natural mothers, about who was parenting her child. This consigned all involved to their worst imaginings about these things. It often denied adopters information that would have reassured them and prepared them better for parenting their adopted child. For example, at that time when academic genetic and nature/nurture cautions predominated, adoptees' childish misdemeanours or appropriate adolescent challenges were frequently misconstrued as more ominous signs of unfortunate genetic unfolding. Misunderstanding and misapprehensions compounded. They were hurtful to all.

Additionally, this was an era with less insight into the significance of the intrauterine environment, the perinatal climate, the realities of ruptures of attachment in infancy, the psychological development of the child, adolescent identity issues, family dynamics and the impact of peer and cultural contexts in people's lives. This meant that too many adoptive parents blamed themselves for what were normative child and adolescent struggles in their adopted children, or understanding that these struggles might be overlaid with the appropriate anxieties and questions of any adoptive child.

For some people who were adopted, adoption implied that they were the second choice for those who would have preferred to have had their 'own' children if they could have done so. It also suggested secondary citizenship when they discovered the meaning of the term 'illegitimate' or when subjected to the allied cruel adjectives describing their status. It implied that they might be harbingers of evil influence in their lineage, concealed characteristics that might manifest at any time. In this way, secrecy implied their origin was too shameful to be revealed, that they had been ill and ignominiously begotten, carelessly abandoned, totally rejected, tainted and containing defective traits that made them dangerous or unlovable. The fact that excessive diligence was exercised in eradicating all means of tracing their natural mother or their family of origin implied that either they, their mother or that family held horrors too terrible to be told.

For when they were denied the dignity of their entitlement to their personal past, to their medical history and their right to know who they were, from whom they came, in what circumstances and by whom and why the decision that they be adopted was taken, their personal identity was expunged. This erased not only their identity, but their family history. It expelled them from their family of origin and their entitlement to access to it.

Secrecy is the source of more pathology than most of the stories it conceals. But the secrecy surrounding adoption prohibited many adoptees from asking questions of their adoptive parents, lest that would imply rejection of their 'rescuers'. Imagination, the substitute for information, often constructed stories of epic nature or grandiose generosity to account for their adoption. This made the routine reality more difficult for those who would later, with difficulty, and despite opposition, manage to track down and take by surprise birth parents ill-prepared for the sudden appearance of an adult child last seen in the throes of a terrible time in their lives.

Adoption in the distant past also condemned most birth mothers to ignorance of the outcome of their decision. For some this fed their worst fears. For others it allowed them to retain their fervent hopes that their child had received a better life than they, at that time, could have provided. For many it ensured a life of guilt, grief and guardianship of a secret that could never be shared.

Many birth mothers feared their children would not understand with what sacrificial love they had relinquished them. Many annually remembered their own child's birthday, wondering what their child might look like on that day: with what colour hair, what depth in their eyes, what happiness in their hearts and whether they would also think of them with love, or anger, sadness, yearning, indifference, rejection or unanswered questioning about why they had been 'given away'.

But adoption is changing and the most overt example of that change has been the National Adoption Contact Preference Register, facilitating contact between those people who were adopted in the past and their natural families when they mutually registered their desire for such connection or reconnection with each other.

It is not just that adoption practices are different today. Society too has changed in the half century since the first Irish Adoption Act. Many of the 42,000 children formally adopted since then are adults now, informing future adoption practices by their experiences as adoptees. Many have discovered brothers, sisters and cousins whose existence or identity was previously concealed.

From almost 1,500 adoption orders in 1967, there were much fewer domestic adoptions of Irish children in so-called 'stranger' adoptions whereby couples take total legal responsibility for other people's children and birth mothers relinquished all legal, access and information rights to their children. Additionally, kinship fostering and kinship adoption and the range of domestic circumstances from which children may be adopted are expanding. The 'best interests of the child' has become more than an abstract ideological aspiration as new forms of domestic adoption prioritise the needs of the individual child.

Research is revisiting and revisioning earlier adoption formats. Standardisation of practices, policies, procedures and practitioner training is advancing. There has been a steady increase in inter-country adoptions since the Adoption Act of 1990, which has helped expand understanding of the complexity of adoption for all. Adoptive couples have enriched their definition of their parenthood to include warm appreciation for the ethnicity, culture, circumstances and eventual cultural reconnection their child may require.

International research suggests that, when it is appropriate and possible, it is best for children to be brought up by their birth family and that adoption should therefore be 'open' because in most instances (not all) that is best for children. Open adoption refers to the continuum of communication amongst members of the adoption triad: adoptive parents, adoptees and birth parents. But levels of openness may still range from the closed confidential cut-off of former times to mediated contact, prescribed contact or fully disclosed relationships; there are also variations in commencement of contact, frequency, intensity, duration and degree.

While openness remains dependent on the wishes of adoptive parents rather than being legislatively prescribed, many natural mothers will not allow their babies to be adopted for fear of 'losing' access to them during their growing years.

But despite these remaining difficulties, the landscape of adoption has changed. Much is now known about what went wrong in a society that penalised single birth mothers, snatched their children, coerced their consent to adoption, kept their off-spring in ignorance of their identity and frequently gave trauma-tised children to adoptive couples, some of whom were themselves traumatised by their own experiences of stillbirth, miscarriages, infertility or grief for the loss of their idealised child.

Much is now known about the distress experienced by adoptive parents when difficulties arose; their acute sense of responsibility for the adopted child, their guilt when accident, ill-ness or emotional distress occurred in that child or in those instances where their biological children were angry or envious of adopted intruders into their lives.

More is understood about adoptive parents' ambivalence when couples without children adopt only to find that an unex-pected pregnancy follows closely upon the adoption after those years of waiting for a child. And there is greater understanding of the identity angst and existential isolation retained by many adopted children that can continue throughout their lives.

The original psychological aridity of adoption produced thousands of birth mothers demented by grief and large numbers of their adult 'children' in subsequent search of them. Birth fathers did not even feature in the past, their names unrecorded on birth certificates and in the narratives of their children's lives. The alter-ation of birth certificates, of identifying documents, the dis-appearance of files, obstruction of search and reunion efforts, and the pain caused to those in whose best interests adoption was designed to serve, has finally been heard. The past is now being listened to. Unfortunately, in this process some former adoptive parents have felt demonised as co-conspirators in these sad circumstances rather than being understood simply as people who wished to provide a home for a child and a child for their home or to become a family because nature had denied them that chance.

In this millennium, yet another Irish past is being healed. In so doing, one group is often blamed. But it is not right to right a wrong by making another wrong. It is therefore important to remember the many children cherished, nurtured and loved within adoption, those for whom their parents *were* their adoptive parents and they in turn their children, those who received the love contained in the words: 'not flesh of my flesh nor bone of my bone, but still miraculously my own, never forget for a single minute, you didn't grow under my heart, but in it.'

FAMILY STRESS:
WEAPON OF
MALE DESTRUCTION

What brings a statesman to his knees? What defeats the insuperable power? What buckles the man? What quenches his courage and conquers him? What is the weapon of male destruction? Why the family, of course!

According to Labour Peer Melvyn Bragg, family factors may have caused British Prime Minister Tony Blair to consider an early resignation.

This announcement was made on the eve of the publication of Blair's wife Cherie Booth's book *The Goldfish Bowl*, which has been co-authored with Lord Bragg's wife, Cate Haste. The book examines the lives of spouses and families of former British Prime Ministers from Anthony Eden to the Blairs' own family life.

The announcement of the impact of family considerations on Blair may surprise those who construed the Prime Minister's less lively demeanour and ageing strain as rumination on the ethical exigencies of his pre-emptive war in Iraq. Not so. Neither invasion nor retaliation, neither the David Kelly tragedy and investigation nor even potential political annihilation made Blair falter.

As popularity waned, the tabloids turned, party members quit, credibility died and no spin could disguise the tactical *ruse de guerre* surrounding the war, Blair appeared obdurate.

But what man, however heroic, armoured, gladiatorial, stoic and unquenchable, does not buckle before the invasion of family concerns? It is not the foreign foe but domestic stress that invades the lives of men. It would seem that Blair is no exception. This is the challenge for today's man.

As more men and women struggle with the work–life balance, corporate accommodation to family life and statutory and non-statutory family-friendly arrangements are high on the agenda of employee mental and psychological health. The days of the 'long-hours' work culture must be numbered if family life is to survive and domestic caring and sharing is to become the equal province of working men and women. Prime ministers are not exempt.

Modern men in power are learning what women have always known. There is no life, no occupation, no ministry and no role more onerous than the parental one. Nothing preoccupies like parenting. So momentous is the parenting task that Aldous Huxley in *Brave New World* referred to 'the appalling dangers of family life'. Now there was a man who knew that creating a Utopian society was chickenfeed compared to the vicissitudes of family life.

Family stress is the ultimate stress. It is not external to the self. It is something you live. You live in it and with it, beside it and around it because some stress is inevitable in the complex life-cycle stages that occur in lives dedicated to family life.

Running government is easy. What woman could not run the family seamlessly if she had at her disposal ministers for trans-port, education, finance, health, planning, justice and defence and a cohort of attendants to advise her and remind her of each daily schedule?

Women (and more recently and increasingly, men) who work at home do the driving, supervise study and juggle the money. They provide total health care: physical, psychological, occupational therapy, physiotherapy and nutrition. They know more about budget deficits and how to survive them, fiscal rectitude and sometimes about poor appreciation for investment.

Think of the immediate planning decisions required to allocate space fairly to applicants amidst the cries of competing siblings, of different temperaments, with diverse requirements, at different ages.

Justice and law are not abstract in family life, where there is daily enforcement and where women have traditionally known that punishment and incarceration are inferior to restorative justice. In family life, justice is everything.

As for immigration and asylum seekers – no parent of an adolescent has not on many occasions with limited notice and minimal investigation of the merits of the case provided equal living standards to migrants.

Domestic defence is a fine art. Every mother knows that when battle is threatened, when factions divide and when war talk begins, then that is the time for diplomacy. Peace is not gained by threat. It is not gained by attacking the enemy. It is not won by power and might, but by understanding and discussion. The culprit is not taught by punishing the group, by threat or harshness.

Negotiation means giving each side an opportunity to express its fear, its hurt and its concerns. Gentleness wins more wars than assault. Possessions are unimportant in the currency of family. Giving in to the more vulnerable, the more needy child is sometimes the more noble path, while behavioural breaches benefit by firm and fair attention.

In a changing world, the family has changed. In the past there were more public figures than public families. Prime ministers' wives were primarily conspicuous by their absence. Most retained their family homes as retreats. Much parenting was done *in abstentia* by provision of nannies followed by an expensive public boarding school education.

What distinguished the Blairs was that they typified many modern families: the vibrant, successful professional couple with separate opinions, different styles, dual careers and hands-on parenting, the working mother encountering the usual jubilation and exhaustion of a new baby, parents dealing with children and adolescents within the landscape of political life.

The occasions in which Cherie Blair spoke spontaneously as a woman or mother, bought living accommodation for her son, chose friends or alliances less convivial to political life or simply celebrated her fiftieth birthday crossed the domestic divide into the public arena. Of course this attracted attention and must have evoked family strain.

The chronicles of men's achievements rarely include their fortitude and sensitivity in the face of family life. It should. Men who succumb to family need are real men. They are wise men to be admired, not despised.

For what keeps the world safe is when men remember their families and truly participate in family life. When they look at their sons and will send no son to battle, when they hold their babies and become attuned to child care, when they sit with a sick infant and understand health policy and when they watch a daughter grow they ensure that policy protects her, her equality, her person, her definition.

At the end of the day, family need is not a weapon of male destruction. Deprivation of family is. To provide men with equal opportunity to be with their children may be their liberation from the subjugation of the role of sole breadwinner, with its past exclusion from the emotional domain of family life.

Creon in Sophocles' *Antigone* says, 'Of course you cannot know a man completely, his character, his principles, sense of judgment, not till he's shown his colours, ruling the people, making laws.' I think he was wrong. You cannot know a man completely until you have seen how he respects his wife, loves his sons, cherishes his daughters, protects his parents and translates this knowledge through personal and emotional life into social policy, corporate practice and political will.

SALE OF THE
FAMILY HOME

The sale of the family of origin home is more than a monetary transaction. It is an emotional event. It is one for which people usually find themselves psychologically unprepared, which is why so many adults are surprised by how sad they feel when the family home is put up for sale.

The psychological effect of the sale of the family of origin home does not feature much in the literature on life-cycle family transitions that require preparation, support and resolution. But it should, because the emotions for adult children that accompany the sale of 'their' family home are often surprisingly intense. The house into which you were born, in which you grew up, where attachments were imprinted, memories embossed, childhood conducted, adolescence encountered and adulthood first ventured is the emotional storehouse of one's personal narrative and family history. Selling this home is often experienced as akin to erasure of one's former self, or at least the location in which one's earlier self was formed.

Home is more than a house. The family of origin house is the ultimate home. Always referred to as 'home', regardless of travel, time, distance or circumstances, it is a place one may depart from but never leave. It is a place that must be vacated voluntarily, with right of return in times of trouble and triumph. It is the place that one is 'from'.

Perhaps this is why severance from the family home brings such transgenerational psychic angst, that it continues even across extensive geographical and time lines. This may be why, for example, millions of Americans, children, grandchildren and great-grandchildren, descendants of emigrants whose rupture with their Irish home place was painful, feel compelled to return to Ireland on their behalf. Because regardless of where one creates subsequent homes, the family of origin home remains the descriptive starting point for one's story of one's life. Where you are 'from' is where you grew up and perhaps one remains a 'blow in' elsewhere forever.

The family home is therefore more than a place. It is a state of mind. Those with unhappy memories of it rarely leave them behind and those with happy childhood memories return to its psychological asylum ever after. Archive of the past, eidetic storehouse of images, of grandparents when they were alive, of one's parents when they were lithe and young, brothers and sisters through babyhood and childhood, aunts, uncles, cousins, friends and family pets in their former manifestations: the family home houses these psychological phantoms. They roam our lives with their presence, provide psychological continuity, an arc from past to present, a continuum of connection from the present into the future.

Cradle of consciousness and developmental domain, the family home contains our first selves, our pre-verbal perceptions, the ground upon which first steps were taken, the place where the diminutive details of childhood observation were made, site of sibling relationships, seminal memories and the wandering ghosts of our own childhood selves.

It is in the family home that every time we return with Proustian passion, we rediscover our most meticulous memories. We remember the crack on an ornament, the odd chipped china cup in the press, the repetitive pattern of wallpaper counted nightly as accompaniment to sleep and waking and wakefulness. We remember the line on a ceiling, depth of wardrobe, fragrance of linen, softness of a pillow, sheen and silkiness of a quilt, tickle of candlewick, hang of curtains, fragrance of cushions, mustiness of books, texture of couch, length of a table, flicker of fire, glow from heater and the scaled sounds of piano practice in another room.

The murmur of voices, tedium of homework, repetition of verse, recitation of tables, the ritual of evening, drawing of curtains, shutting of doors, scraping of chairs, rotation of records when their sound was spent, buzz of transistor, televised anthem at close of evening, household creaks and squeaks, noises of a past life.

Who can forget the stirring of morning, smell of porridge, slants of light measuring the day, the path through the garden and the mysteries it contained, the activity of life in, around, about, above, beneath and beside the house? Archive of our first imaginings and our most visceral reflections, the family home's shapes, sounds and smells infuse our psyche and allow us every time we return to renew our senses with these visions and voices from the past.

The family home, therefore, is an emotional abode. It is a psychological province. It hallmarks its occupants with an indelible identity. This is home. This is where you come from. This is what made and shaped you. Site of conception, cradle of childhood, springboard of adulthood, kingdom of belonging: while the family home remains, the past is preserved.

But it cannot remain forever. How it is bequeathed or sold, when and why, may determine the emotional response its sale evokes. When the childhood home comes under the hammer, a blow is struck in the heart of grown adults that is akin to being abandoned and orphaned.

The family feuds that so often erupt, surprisingly, inexplicably and intensely, are rarely about money or about a house, but about being cherished, about finality, sale of the past, irretrievability of that time, inability to change it or retain it, and about how much one was loved in that place long ago.

CHRISTMAS EXPECTATIONS: FESTIVE FICTION

Christmas rarely lives up to its Christmas card image. The idealised family is shown gathered beside the tree and around the fire; adults united, children contented, slumbering dogs, glittering gifts and nearby a table laden with culinary excellence. Through the gleaming window can be seen the glow of snow, a top-hatted snowman, an observant robin, a distant church steeple and a frozen lake upon which gleeful skating youth celebrate the festivities as children toboggan with abandonment down a nearby hill.

Beautiful. But traditional images display abstract aspirations rather than ordinary family life.

Such pictures of perfection, portrayed since childhood and embedded in the subconscious of every adult, induce feelings of inadequacy and guilt in those who believe, however subliminally, that this is how life is lived. Since no family can live up to this Christmas card ideal, all families must fall short of it.

For pictures are static. Families are not. Families are real. They are vibrant, living, evolving, dynamic, intense inter-relationships that cannot be reduced to one printed depiction of perfection. For any rational person examining the traditional Christmas scene must ask the following questions: who dressed the children and fed the dog, lit the fire, decorated the tree, wrapped the presents, prepared the punch, built the snowman, cooked the meal and financed the festivities? What normal family could do all that and not be stressed?

Myths surround family gatherings at Christmas time: that old rivalries will disappear, that tensions will not occur, that emotions will not emerge and that there will not be moments of anxiety, anger, sadness and hurt as well as those of closeness, sibling synchrony and family harmony.

Going home for Christmas is special, whether from distant places or down the road. Having a family home to go to, a family with whom to celebrate at Christmas time, are amongst life's distinctive gifts. Preparing for that visit lends additional purpose and meaning to the Christmas season, the exhaustion of shopping and the trials of travel. Being amongst 'one's own' on Christmas morning protects the individual from loneliness, isolation and disconnection from the world.

Going home for Christmas is what people usually want to do. But going home also requires realistic expectations to avoid psychological distress when festive fiction is uncovered and normal festive frictions occur.

For the miracle of Christmas is not that perfection is found in families, but that despite imperfection this is the place that most people still want to be and return to annually despite their disappointments of the previous year. It is not that adult siblings morph into ideal people, but that they stay reassuringly the same loving, gentle, robust, maddening, argumentative and competitive people they have always been. It is not that families sit in static serenity, but that they are scattered around the house. It is not that the floor is tidy, but that it is littered with ripped wrapping paper, crumpled crackers and gaudy paper hats, half-eaten sweets and dog hairs. It is not that children are silent, but that they are eager, energised and excited. It is not that the kitchen is ordered, but that it is filled with the clutter of utensils, dishes, bowls, plates, pots and busyness and half-drunk glasses of wine. It is not that the décor is designer ordained, but that there is a welcome in it for all who call that is warm.

The family Christmas is no more perfect than a stable was the perfect place for a divine incarnation to begin. Yet the family brings people from near and far annually, to celebrate life at every level, the ordinary and the godly. It seems to be where we belong.

Coming Out

———

Despite the enormous cultural and ideological changes ascribed to twenty-first-century life, most parents retain straightforward aspirations for their children.

They hope that they will progress 'normally' through the stages of childhood and adolescence into adulthood. That *en route* they will acquire a small cohort of good and loyal friends so that they will not be lonely, that they will have a social life, confidantes in times of worry and co-celebrants in times of joy.

They hope they will achieve academic standards consistent with their ability and obtain sufficient educational credentials to enjoy employment in adequately remunerative work that is of interest and fulfilment.

Finally, they hope that they will love someone who will love, understand and be faithful to them, that in time, if they so wish, they will get married, have children and that, in turn, they will one day observe their own children achieve these life-cycle stages and satisfactions in life. This is 'health, wealth and happiness': life's pattern woven, seasonal assuredness, transgenerational continuity guaranteed.

It is not in the life plan of parents that their son or daughter should one day announce that he or she is gay. But an estimated, although somewhat controversial, 'research' figure of 10 per cent of parents may one day hear this news. Whether this statistic is exaggerated or not, the fact is that there are many parents who will learn that their children are gay. From whom they gain this information, how parents are told, what they are told and the expectations of them when they are told are crucial to this 'coming out' event. Indeed, whether or not their children can 'trust' their parents with this information continues to be an ongoing issue and it is one that is not always well resolved, sometimes being blurted out on unsuspecting parents, sometimes being concealed forever because it seems that it cannot be told.

This is summarised succinctly in writer Alan Bennett's book *Untold Stories* when he tells of the only time the issue of his sexual orientation was mooted by his father, with the question, 'You're not one of those, are you?', to which there was no appropriate reply but agreement that he was not whatever 'one of those' implied. With such questions that do not ask but plead not to be told, what other answer could there be?

One expectation that can sever the relationship between parents and child is if the news is announced to parents with anticipation of immediate acceptance. Given that the majority of gay people come to their own realisation that they are gay over an extended time period and often after their own initial tortuous rejection before adjustment to the reality of their sexual orientation, it is unrealistic to expect parents to receive the news with nonchalance. It is not insignificant news. It is unlikely to be welcome news because parents do not wish their children to have any additional difficulties imposed upon them. It is news that takes at least a little while to process and accept.

Parents who learn that their child is gay may experience overwhelming emotion and many parents who consult clinicians for help in adjusting to this information describe it thus. The news shatters the life plan, upturns aspirations, invokes enormous guilt and may conjure up the worst and most extreme images of a debaucherous, flamboyant and hazardous lifestyle, while an avalanche of pejorative terms may come to mind, terms with which they do not wish their child to be burdened.

The news may arouse extreme ambivalence, plunging parents into the extraordinarily complex position of hating the 'group' of which their much-loved child has declared him or herself a member. It may engender fears that being 'gay' resulted from their failure to protect their child from a sexual abuse in childhood or that it is due to some other grim parental fault. They may wonder if they provided adequate role models, if this is a genetic inheritance, why this has come about, and what if anything they could have done to have spared their child this difference in a world that is not tolerant of difference, even if it be more tolerant than it was in former times.

It worries parents to contemplate their gay child alone, without love in their adult life, but it terrifies them even more to imagine a gay 'partner' lurking in the background who may be intimate in some aberrant way with their offspring. Every extreme hurtful stereotype may emerge in the moment parents are told. This needs to be understood.

Some parents react less extremely but with profound sadness for the loneliness and social exclusion their child may face, for the grandchildren that will never be born and for the life their child will lead in the shadow of prejudice and discrimination, for the pretence they may require if they conceal their orientation or the persecution they may endure if they disclose it.

Almost all parents wonder if something can be done to 'cure' the condition or ensure that it is an irremediable reality rather than a temporary lifestyle choice. Families may react emotionally as brothers and sisters respond, frequently with entirely unpredicted reactions. Rejection may come from the sibling most expected to support, acceptance from the least likely family member. Same-sex siblings may fear the disclosure casts doubt upon their own sexuality and family disputes can erupt between those who support or reject the situation.

While these are understandable family reactions, a gay son who has just bared his soul, disclosed his sexuality and revealed his identity may experience them as an intense rejection of who and what he is. To seek a 'cure' is to say that he is 'diseased' and to reject reality is to deny his identity.

To risk 'coming out' to that potential intensity of family responses is an act of extreme courage and profound need on the part of the person who is gay. It is a measure of how important it is to the gay person to continue as an accepted family member and to retain parental love and regard irrespective of sexual orientation.

It is a test of whether love is conditional or unconditional.

It is a test that can have tragic consequences if a son or daughter is ostracised or denied or put in a position that they believe they can never tell their parents what their orientation is. Therefore, how parents respond, what they say in response and the tone of their reply are crucial.

Regardless of inner turmoil, the best outward response parents can make is a reassuring embrace and expression of concern for the turmoil their child must have experienced in order to come to this point.

WORDS

Introduction

With the 'Word' the world began. Words shape our world. From the first tentative human sound to our final faltering utterance, words surround, circumscribe, delineate and describe our world and our place within it.

With words our arrival is announced; by obituary, death confirmed. Words name the child, aspirations are articulated and the process of learning a language and languaging a life begins. Think of the celebration at the utterance of a child's first word and the pride when first the letters and then an entire, recognisable, wonderful word appears on the page, printed painstakingly by a toddler hand.

Reading and writing are the gateways to knowledge, the portals to pedagogy and rites of passage to intellectual life. Words carry cultural meaning and worth, encircle prejudices or enlarge understanding. Life stages are marked by the words that are spoken, the vows that are made, the promises inferred and the words conferred. Secular ceremonies and religious rites require words with which to bestow status, recognise new stages or renew obligations.

In the wider world of words, war does not 'occur', it is 'declared'. The art of diplomacy is dedication to the delicacy of words. Words may acclaim or defame, may incite or excite, may soothe or smooth over the edges of life. Words once local are global, and just as in times past oral traditions were threatened by print, print in turn is now threatened by image. But no image can ever out-speak the spell of the printed word for those who love the polished perfection of those precise descriptors of life.

Entire professions are built upon words: the novelist, the poet, the journalist inhabit the vaults of vocabulary, digging deep in the lexicons of imagination amongst the thesaurus of times present and past, storing, selecting, shining, extracting, considering, choosing, committing to the page the phonemes, gnomes and glossemes of communication in wondrous polyphonic, prosodic, pleonastic sequential arrays of words!

There is musicality in words, langue *and* parole, *the linguistics of living, the lilt of words, their intonation, liveliness, contours and cadences. They stir all senses with their shape, texture, tenor, modulation, pitch, inflection and energy, while in libraries and publishers' warehouses and wherever books congregate there is the indescribable smell of the printed word upon the page.*

And what of poetry: the ode, idyll, sonnet, lyric, lament? What of the epics of human imagination and the onomatopoeia of life? In Sigmund Freud's introductory lectures on psychoanalysis, he said that 'words were originally magic and to this day they have retained much of their ancient magical power'. And it is so, for they sing their Siren song and all is lost for those of us who love them.

Grammatolatry, the worship of words, is an irrevocable obsession. That is why these final articles attempt to convey the alchemy of that affinity with the spoken or written word for those of you who share this sanctified affliction.

Whether that be addiction to the rich spectrum of colourful language, the polysemy of popular parlance or the vertiginous vagaries and vibrancy of the vernacular; whether it be the gnomes and aphorisms of affective life found in the proverbs of our inner souls and national psyche, or even the pleonastic, fustian extravaganza of playfulness with words occasionally, rapaciously indulged in in this book: love of language is its own tyranny and its own reward.

But the ultimate affective affliction is that of bibliophilia, a condition reserved for those most floridly affected with that incurable condition and insatiable desire for books.

It is a divine affliction, this 'light behind a written word', as you, gentle readers and fellow sufferers, well know!

Do You
Suffer from
Bibliophilia?

Whenever there is a book launch, there gather a congregation of people in that bookshop who are instantaneously united in shared possessive and obsessive love of books.

This manifests itself in their compassionate acceptance of each other's eccentricities. They understand the urge to sidle along shelves, seeking sightings of old friends or the possibility of new literary acquaintances hidden amongst them.

They see no aberration in holding a book in gentle adulation, laying hands lovingly upon its cover, opening its pages to turn them with individual idolisation as familiar words are scanned. They recognise the need to murmur well-known stanzas, to repeat these cantos of childhood, revelations of adolescence, source of adult illumination and ecstasy of older age.

Book lovers understand the lifelong odyssey of edification with the printed word, because they themselves are engaged in this paradoxical quest: seeking the ineffable in the word, wisdom in the written and meaning by communing with many other minds.

Bibliophiles appreciate that in a bookshop crowded with their kind there will be more greedy glances towards the books than towards the complimentary food and wine. For books are nurture, elixir, inebriant and sustenance for those who love them. Without them, the mind is parched and the soul declines.

There is an excitement amongst book lovers at a book launch. This is the birth of a new 'edition' to what is written. Bibliophiles gather to congratulate and celebrate those who conceived the story, germinated the ideas, laboured in its delivery and now launch this new literary life into the world.

Celebrating books is more than understanding the power of prose, the educative potential and imaginative transformation of reading. Readers know the excitement of beginning a new book: accompanying new friends through lives, times, experiences, possibilities and opportunities that the world outside that book might never give.

We live alternative lifetimes within the written word.

Readers comprehend the consolation found in characters that share their existential angst, inexplicable emotions or irrational ruminations in this indecipherable life. They know that reading a book means entering a relationship: being ready to appreciate what it wishes to reveal, patient as its narrative unfolds and faithful to its final word.

In fact, what causes most readers' reluctance to turn those closing pages in a book is the rupture of relationship; eviction from the fictional life, grief at the loss of those characters from whose future lives one is being excluded ever more. There is the sense of abandoning or being forsaken by good friends, those who have excited curiosity, anger, awe or empathy, sympathy, ardour and admiration. All are now gone.

Stories are often told about our much-loved late novelist John

McGahern, who as a child remained so absorbed when reading that only extreme measures by his sisters, such as removing the chair upon which he sat, were sufficient to, as he put it, 'wake out of the book'. Readers know that experience of being elsewhere with a book, of turning that last page and being disoriented, of straddling two worlds: unwilling to leave one to re-enter the other.

Our books are precious things. Many people would give away all their possessions rather than lend a favourite book. Who has not panicked at the possibility of entrusting a valued volume to the care and custody of another? Who has not witnessed the cruel removal of a copy from its cradle in the bookcase, leaving a gaping space in place of that book's rightful abode? In the words of Charles Lamb, English essayist and critic, borrowers of books are 'mutilators of collections, spoilers of the symmetry of shelves, and creators of odd volumes'. But Lamb misses the emotional point, which is the bibliophile's fear that the beloved book may be ill treated and return to its owner with dog-eared accusation that it was ever released into such irreverent hands.

Indeed, friendship may be measured by the willingness of friends to lend each other books and the zenith of friendship amongst bibliophiles is reached when they voluntarily reach into their own bookshelves to suggest they lend the other a book to read.

Anne Fadiman in *Ex Libris* recounts how after several years of marriage, she and her husband having lived together, loved together and had a child together, dared to enter into a marital act of far greater intimacy than any in which they had previously engaged. That was to share and divide their individual libraries and to amalgamate their books. The climax of this act of ultimate commitment was reached when they agreed to discard some duplicates. For love between bibliophilic spouses must surely be when they relinquish a favourite book to make shelf space for the other.

But the definitive diagnosis of bibliophilia is the behaviour of the bibliophile deprived of any reading matter. It is then that the addiction attains its most acute, agitated and florid form. Written word deprivation is a debilitating dispossession. Travelling book lovers who have found themselves in hotel rooms late at night without their books recount regression to repeated reading of the local telephone directory while admissions of reading cereal boxes at breakfast time have also been recorded.

Should these symptoms sound familiar, you are a true bibliophile, a condition for which, fortunately, there is no cure.

THE VERNACULAR

Immigrants have much to adjust to emotionally. Even before departure there is the dilemma of whether to stay in one's own country or go to another, anxiety about what lies ahead and the strongest emotion of all, that of hope.

To hope is to expect. To confront one's hope is to face the possibility of that hope being unfulfilled. Moving to another country and hoping it will bring what one desires means that hope will be either achieved or quashed; the promise of a better life will be rewarded or thwarted, one's dreams will become reality or reality will be a disappointment. There is more than a geographical journey ahead for those who leave home for another life. It is an emotional odyssey, a social voyage, a psychological excursion and a linguistic expedition.

There are risks involved in moving to another culture: of not being accepted, of not fitting in, of not being welcomed, of making inadvertent cultural errors. There may be fundamental ideological differences to be accommodated, ways of living, modes of dress, home décor, choices of food and leisure activities.

There are bureaucratic burdens to be endured, endless paperwork to authenticate one's identity, legitimacy and entitlement to work. Different work ethics may inform work practice and it is not easy to know what is expected, what one may expect and how to define one's rights and roles in a different country.

Finally, there may be fear of loneliness, of being excluded, of being ghettoised amongst one's compatriots, of being tolerated, of being resented, of being scapegoated or of being unable to understand what one is meant to do in order to fit in.

Even when welcomed warmly, the immigrant has to discover what the local person takes for granted, such as how to respond to invitations, what time to arrive and leave, what jokes are permitted and what subjects are strictly taboo. Simply joining friends for a pint can involve a rigmarole of rounds that is incomprehensible to those who do not know how the system works, and frustrating for those who do not believe it is a sensible way of socialising.

Language barriers abound. Language proficiency does not mean that the immigrant understands the native idiom, or what is colloquially called 'the vernacular'. Language in its articulation is local and few idiomatic idiosyncrasies can compete with the manner in which the English language has been appropriated by the Irish, amalgamated with the richness of that tongue and been uttered ever since in its own unique manner that contains the social encryptions of what we mean, what we really mean and what we really, really mean. It takes a lifetime to decipher that.

Entry to the workforce is particularly difficult for immigrants working in the mental health professions, particularly psychiatry, psychology and psychotherapy, because they are professions that depend upon linguistic skill and where literal interpretation of local idiom may either lead to laughter or litigation depending upon the client. One must have sympathy for the new psychologist who misinterpreted the Dublin adolescent's declaration that his ma was wrecking his head as a disclosure of physical ill treatment and that the ma who ate the head off her kids was not engaging in some bizarre form of cannibalism. Being ossified does not refer to the condition of one's bones; to loaf has nothing to do with bread. Mitch is not a name but a form of truancy. To bang on about something means boring people while the exclamation 'bang on' does not mean to hit repeatedly but to be absolutely correct. Acting the maggot is not imitation of larvae but a form of nonsensical behaviour.

To receive a referral for someone who has fallen off the wagon is confusing, particularly when a wagon also appears to be a derogatory term for a female. A scrubber is not someone engaged in domestic cleaning and Janey Mac is no more a person than Holy Joe, while the term out of sight, out of mind does not refer to someone suffering either from blindness or mental incapacity.

Apart from the obvious cliché that those in search of *craic* are not seeking illegal substances, the immigrant has to learn that having a gargle is not using mouthwash, that an old cod is not out-of-date fish, that declaring something thick is a cognitive rather than a physical evaluation, the full shilling is not a financial statement, something deadly is neither dangerous nor deceased and making a holy show of oneself is not a religious demonstration.

The dictionary is of little use to the immigrant confronting our polysemous parlance, for we are a people who have always expressed the ineffable through euphemism and the effable in inexpressible ways, resorting to and augmenting the letter 'f' when other modes of utterance fail.

The Irish may be difficult to interpret, but most of us are glad that you have chosen to come to our country. Or to put it another way, take heart, dear immigrants, for although it's brutal trying to figure out what we are on about, it's deadly when you do and it's massive that you're here.

Colourful Language

────────────

Colour plays an important role in our lives. Whether we pay conscious or unconscious attention to it, colour influences our emotional, behavioural, cognitive and social worlds. It exerts an influence on our identities, our affiliations, our daily attire, our social messages, our emotional mood and our memories. It is also our first gender marker.

From birth, the child is gender defined by traditional pink or blue and the wrapped gifts, cards and flowers that greet his or her arrival. Children's own engagement with colour is intense. They love it, which is why they choose bright, bold, primary colours when depicting their world and every advertiser knows that the child-targeted television programme or product would be ineffectual without rainbow combinations of the brightest hues.

Women have also, perhaps, been more socially constructed by colour than men. Consider the symbolic polarities of white and red in relation to women. The social commentary contained in 'and the bride wore white' conveyed more than her choice of garment, while the 'scarlet woman' in times past was condemned to a life outside 'agreeable society' and the social exclusions embodied in that term.

Social exclusion was also contained in the notion of those of 'noble birth' with 'blue blood' coursing through their veins, as distinguished from the rest of us lesser mortals who had to contend with blood of common red.

Adjectives abound for colour choices in clothes, with positive or negative ascriptions contained therein. For example, depending on culture, fashion and traditions, the presence or absence of colour in clothes will either be designated garish or discreet, loud or understated. The conservative view that 'less is more' prevails, unless, perversely, it is outrageously flamboyant, in which case it may be described as 'devastatingly daring'.

A woman's choice of vivid colours in clothes may therefore be termed brassy, gaudy and tasteless or be interpreted as vibrant and innovative. More two-toned 'business' choices of classic wear acquire the descriptors modest, tasteful and reserved unless they are regarded as dull, dreary or monotonous, a double-bind that women have to negotiate for each occasion in their lives.

Men have traditionally been dismissed as colour blind, a designation they now challenge in colour combinations that brighten their own and women's lives. The architectural, decorator/ designer terms that now invade almost every living space provide a staggering number of differentiations along the colour continuum so that you need to know your chartreuse from your fuchsia, khaki from ochre, annatto from ecru and crimson from cochineal, lest you be left in that vivid shade, mortified by ignorance.

Physiologically and emotionally we equate feeling unwell with being pale, off colour, the onset of nausea as turning green. And who of a certain vintage does not remember yellow submarine, purple haze or whiter shade of pale? Being of light-hearted, lucky disposition is in the pink, low mood is feeling blue, anger makes us see red, in the throes of foul feelings we experience a black mood, while the Dublin expression for acute embarrassment brings forth the phrase 'I was scarlet', a wonderful descriptor of that awful suffusion of colour that we all occasionally experience when we have made some mortifying social gaffe.

Morally, good and evil are polarised, with lights of dazzling whiteness around benign visitations, while dark apparitions are clad in the 'black cloak of night'. Yet at a cognitive level we acknowledge that few situations are entirely black or white, nor should we polarise ourselves at those perspectival extremes. And while grey is hardly associated with cheerfulness, it does at least imply compromise, though some would suggest that it is simply a dilution of everyone's point of view.

And when people look back through Ireland's history, it is not just in historical or economic terms that 'dark times' are referenced, but is also due to the fact that the photograph albums and footage of times past were dreary in their achromatic dullness. For many of us, all records of our early lives were flat, fixed in that monotone of memory and in our memory of monotone.

Nationality is conceptualised and primarily visualised through colour; a flag is not a coloured cloth. To insult a nation's colours is to insult its people, while the county colours, the sports team colours, affirm the degree to which we assume team identities through colour and defend those colours to the death.

And while we may occasionally grin at our exploitation of the stereotypical imagery of Ireland, our appropriation of green, the 'wearing o' it', its 'forty shades', its good luck potential and our green-velvet-suited leprechauns, we are, ironically, lagging in our efforts to be that other 'green' of environmental respect.

We may have surpassed the primitive imagery of those other 'little green men' through whom we once imagined 'alien' life descending from circular ships, yet we still discriminate and demonise that which we do not understand on the basis of colour.

Has not atavistic antagonism towards colour of skin not been amongst our most tragic misunderstanding of colour and of the rich diversity and hue of life that we each bring to life's spectrum?

PROVERBS

There is wisdom in proverbs. There is beauty in their message. There is advice behind their brevity: the short, sharp syntax of sagacity with its undeniable chime of truth. Proverbs address every aspect of life. There is recognition in their detail. There is reassurance in their universality. Individually they remind us of the perceptiveness of people about every human condition and context. Collectively they are testament to the accumulated wisdom of the ages and the indomitable wit and wisdom of the human mind.

Psychologists have traditionally been aware of the abstract, analysable, figurative and metaphoric function of proverbs and their capacity to say what cannot otherwise be expressed, or certainly not expressed so succinctly. Family therapists have been fascinated by the degree to which families may appropriate certain maxims as models of family life. For example, 'blood is thicker than water' is an implicit imperative to family members that whatever internal disagreements may abound, you stick by your own and support the clan.

But proverbs also extend to advice about neighbourliness, co-operation and community cohesion (many hands make light work), about interpersonal communications (civility costs no money), about assessments of people (don't judge a book by its cover), about holding one's tongue in social situations (a silent mouth is sweet sounding) and everyday diplomatic interactions (a person's mouth often broke his own nose).

Proverbs caution us about financial management (he that goes a borrowing goes a-sorrowing) and about judicious investment (don't put all your eggs in one basket). They provide a philosophical perspective on wealth (contentment is the greatest of riches) and allied issues of social conscience (as the money bag swells, the heart contracts) and social injustice (a poor man's tale cannot be heard). And who does not find their breath catching at the stark reality contained in that phrase?

But it is in the area of marriage and romantic relationships that adages guide, reassure, caution and admonish us. Sweet is the notion that there is someone for everyone, or that 'every old sock finds an old shoe'; cautionary is the maxim that if you 'marry in haste you repent at leisure'; and how wonderfully anti-ageist is the adage that 'old coals are easiest kindled', affirming that passion is not the exclusive provenance of youth.

Proverbs provide a pastiche of psychological insights in accessible packaging. Many of these seemingly simple sentences have received subsequent scientific verification through psychological and sociological research. For the scope of the proverb is as wide as life. It extends to every facet of existence. With the deceptive semblance of impromptu profundity, proverbs provide immediate action plans. Proverbs guide us through the mundane mechanics of ordinary life, remind us of our mortality and acknowledge our struggle with life's imponderables. They are moral imperatives. Their clarity comforts, and in times of need we make nostalgic returns to those Irish clichés that provided a phrase for every life phase, a sentence for every sentiment, acute observation of the behaviour of people and words of consolation for every occasion.

'The genius, wit and spirit of a nation are discovered in its proverbs,' wrote Francis Bacon. Perhaps despite the clichéd nature of our most familiar phrases, which inevitably 'breed their own contempt', there is still psychological relevance, sociological insight and economic guidance to be found in these words of wit and wisdom today.

The *seanfhocal* of our forefathers and foremothers may have provided them in pre-media and pre-therapy times with informative maxims to guide them. Psychotherapy may not have been available, but the proverb was. Few situations arose for which there was not some proverbial prescription: the solution in a sentence that formed everyday commentary and internal reflection.

Do they have value today? While they may not be spoken aloud in the way they tripped from the tongue of people in the past, their function is not redundant and they continue to hold psychological significance in a new way. They are the emotional vocabulary through which life was once articulated. They contained economic injunctions, health strategies that warned of the inherent dangers of alcohol and idleness, and prescriptions for psychological happiness. They prepared prospective spouses for the realities of life after the dowry was spent. Their philosophical tone excited the imagination of many people who were deprived of the privilege of formal education. They inspired them. Ideas too big for discussion were encapsulated in a phrase.

The distinguished collectors of proverbs show how we gain insight into a society through its proverbs. They say that we can learn what is 'most near and dear' to the hearts of a people, how they interpret honour and dishonour and what their emotional ideologies are, by examining the proverbs they employ. Proverbs are an integral part of our rich Irish oral tradition. They provide insight into our national psyche. While we may regard them as quaint adages of a former era, we might also ask with what superior wisdom have we replaced them.

Perhaps, then, we might remind ourselves that unless we have surpassed these wise old words of another era with psychological interventions that supersede them, that 'people in glass houses shouldn't throw stones'.

*This book is not designed to be a self-help manual, a clinical
work or to provide formal psychological or professional advice.
However, some of the articles explore sensitive issues about
which people may wish to receive further information or assistance.
For that purpose a directory of relevant services and supports
has been compiled.*

*This directory of resources includes a range of organisations
and groups across public and voluntary sectors. It provides basic
information on who they are and how to access them. However,
the directory cannot be, and does not claim to be comprehensive,
and further information about regional and local services may
be obtained through the websites or national branch offices.*

*In providing this list no personal recommendation with regard
to the services listed is made or implied by the author or by the
publishers, and while every effort has been made to ensure that the
information given is accurate and up-to-date, no responsibility can
be taken in the event of errors. Additionally, it is always recommended that in any situation of concern people seek professional
advice, and in relation to health or mental health that they consult
their local general practitioner or health authority.*

Directory of Resources

Adoption Advice Service
Offers information, advice, support and counselling on every aspect of adoption.
Address: Barnardo's, Christchurch Square, Dublin 8
Tel: 01 4530355
Helpline number: 01 4546388 (Thurs 10a.m.–2p.m.)
E-mail: adoption@barnardos.ie
Website: www.barnardos.ie

Age Action Ireland Ltd
Aims to improve quality of life for all older people.
Address: 30/31 Lower Camden Street, Dublin 2
Tel: 01 4756989
Fax: 01 4756011
E-mail: info@ageaction.ie
Website: www.ageaction.ie

Al-Anon Family Groups
Aims to provide help to relatives and friends of problem drinkers.
Address: Al-Anon Information Centre, Room 5, 5 Capel Street, Dublin 1
Tel/Fax: 01 8732699 (fax phone)
Website: www.al-anonuk.org.uk

Alone (A Little Offering Never Ends)
Aims to help older people in need.
Address: No. 1 Willie Bermingham Place, Kilmainham Lane,
Dublin 8
Tel: 01 6791032
E-mail: alone@iol.ie
Website: www.alone.ie

The Alzheimer Society of Ireland
Aims to maximise quality of life for people with Alzheimer's
disease and related dementias, and their carers.
Address: 43 Northumberland Avenue, Dun Laoghaire,
Co. Dublin
Tel: 01 2846616
Fax: 01 2846030
Helpline number: 1800 341341
E-mail: info@alzheimer.ie
Website: www.alzheimer.ie

A.B.C. (Anti-Bullying Centre)
Aims to aid individuals and organisations in the prevention
and reduction of bullying.
Address: Room 3125, Arts Building, Trinity College Dublin,
Dublin 2
Tel: 01 8962573
Website: www.abc.tcd.ie

Aware
Aims to assist individuals and families whose lives are
affected by depression.
Address: 72 Lower Leeson Street, Dublin 2

Tel: 01 6617211
Fax: 01 6617217
Helpline number: 1890 303302 (10a.m.–10p.m.)
E-mail: info@aware.ie
Website: www.aware.ie

The Bereavement Counselling Service
Offers support and counselling to adults and children to enable them to deal with their grief.
Address: Dublin Street, Baldoyle, Dublin 13
Tel/Fax: 01 8391766 (9.15a.m.–1p.m.)
E-mail: bereavement@eircom.net
Website: www.bereavementireland.org

Bethany Bereavement Support Group
Aims to support those who have suffered a loss.
Address: Rathfarnham Parish Centre, Willbrook Road, Rathfarnham, Dublin 14
Tel: 087 9905299
E-mail: bethanysupport@eircom.net
Website: www.bethany.ie

Bodywhys
Offers support, information and understanding for people with eating disorders, their families and friends.
Address: PO Box 105, Blackrock, Co. Dublin
Tel: 01 2834963
Fax: 01 2056959
Helpline number: 1890 200444
E-mail: info@bodywhys.ie
Website: www.bodywhys.ie

The Carers Association
Provides support for family carers and for those receiving care in the home.
Address: 'Prior's Orchard', John's Quay, Kilkenny
Tel: 056 7721424
Fax: 056 7753531
Helpline number: 1800 240724
E-mail: info@carersireland.com
Website: www.carersireland.com

CARI (Children At Risk in Ireland)
Aims to provide therapy for children, young people and families who have been affected by child sexual abuse.
Address: 110 Lower Drumcondra Road, Dublin 9
Tel: 01 8308529
Fax: 01 8306309
Helpline number: 1890 924567 (Mon–Fri, 9.30a.m.–5.30p.m.)
E-mail: helpline@cari.ie
Website: www.cari.ie

Clanwilliam Institute
Aims to provide support, counselling and therapy for families, couples and individuals.
Address: 18 Clanwilliam Terrace, Dublin 2.
Tel: 01 6761363/6762881
Fax: 01 6762800
E-mail: office@clanwilliam.ie
Website: www.clanwilliam.ie

Console
Aims to provide support to those bereaved by suicide.
Address: All Hallows College, Grace Park Road, Drumcondra, Dublin 9
Tel: 01 8574300
Fax: 01 8574310
Helpline number: 1800 201890
E-mail: info@console.ie
Website: www.console.ie

Cúnamh
Aims to provide a pregnancy counselling, adoption and reunion service for birth mothers and adoptees.
Address: 30 South Anne Street, Dublin 2
Tel: 01 6779664
Fax: 01 6770235
E-mail: info@cunamh.com
Website: www.cunamh.com

Cura
Aims to provide a pregnancy and post-abortion counselling service.
Address: 30 South Anne Street, Dublin 2
Tel: 01 6710598
Fax: 01 6710886
Helpline number: 1850 622626
E-mail: curacares@cura.ie

The Dublin Rape Crisis Centre
Provides support to women and men who have experienced rape, sexual assault, sexual harassment and/or childhood sexual abuse.
Address: 70 Lower Leeson Street, Dublin 2
Tel: 01 6614911
Fax: 01 6610873
Freephone: 1800 778888
E-mail: rcc@indigo.ie
Website: www.drcc.ie

Focus Ireland
Aims to advance the right of people-out-of-home to live in a place they call home through quality services, research and advocacy.
Address: 9–12 High Street, Christchurch, Dublin 8
Tel: 01 8815900
Fax: 01 8815950
Helpline number: 1800 724724 (24-hour referral service to Health Board Emergency Number)
E-mail: info@focusireland.ie
Website: www.focusireland.ie

Gingerbread (National Association of Lone Parents)
Aims to enhance the quality of life for families, children and parents facing the future alone.
Address: Carmichael House, North Brunswick Street, Dublin 7
Tel: 01 8146618
Fax: 01 8146619
E-mail: info@gingerbread.ie
Website: www.gingerbread.ie

Gay Switchboard Dublin
Aims to provide confidential information, support or referral to gay men, lesbians, bisexual men/women, their friends and families.
Address: Carmichael House, North Brunswick Street, Dublin 7
Tel: 01 8721055
Fax: 01 8735737
E-mail: info@gayswitchboard.ie
Website: www.gayswitchboard.ie

Grow
Aims to help people who have suffered, or are suffering from, mental health problems.
Address: 167a Capel Street, Dublin 1
Tel: 01 8734029
Fax: 01 8734029
E-mail: info@grow.ie
Website: www.grow.ie

Headway Ireland
Aims to bring about positive change in the lives of those affected by an acquired brain injury.
Address: 1–3 Manor Street Business Park, Manor Street, Dublin 7
Tel: 01 8102066
Fax: 01 8102070
Helpline number: 1890 200278
E-mail: info@headwayireland.ie
Website: www.headwayireland.ie

Irish Society for the Prevention of Cruelty to Children (ISPCC)
Specialises in the prevention of cruelty to children.
Address: 29 Lower Baggot Street, Dublin 2
Tel: 01 6767960
Fax: 01 6789012
Helpline number: 1800 666666
E-mail: ispcc@ispcc.ie
Website: www.ispcc.ie

Irish Cancer Society
Dedicated to eliminating cancer as a major health problem and improving the lives of those living with cancer.
Address: 43–45 Northumberland Road, Dublin 4
Tel: 01 2310500
Fax: 01 2310555
Helpline number: 1800 200700 (Mon–Fri 9a.m.–5p.m., Thursday 9a.m.–7p.m.)
Website: www.cancer.ie

Irish Council for Psychotherapy
Promotes psychotherapy as an independent profession in Ireland and monitors training standards within the profession with the purpose of protecting the public.
Address: 73 Quinn's Road, Shankill, Co. Dublin
Tel: 01 2722105
Fax: 01 2722111
E-mail: amdps@indigo.ie
Website: www.psychotherapy-ireland.com

Irish Friends of the Suicide Bereaved
Aims to support people who have been bereaved by suicide.
Address: The Planning Office, St Finbarr's Hospital, Douglas, Cork
Tel: 021 4316722
E-mail: ifsb@gofree.indigo.ie

Irish Refugee Council
Aims to influence Ireland's policy on asylum-seekers and refugees through research, lobbying and media-influencing.
Address: 88 Capel Street, Dublin 1
Tel: 01 8730042
Fax: 01 8730088
E-mail: refugee@iol.ie
Website: www.irishrefugeecouncil.ie

Irish Sudden Infant Death Association
Offers support to families bereaved by the sudden unexpected death of an infant.
Address: Carmichael House, 4 North Brunswick Street, Dublin 7
Tel: 01 8732711
Fax: 01 8726056
Helpline number: 1850 391391

Irish Wheelchair Association
Aims to provide opportunities for people with physical difficulties to live independently and to participate fully in their community.
Address: Áras Cúchulainn, Blackheath Drive, Clontarf, Dublin 3
Tel: 01 8186400
Fax: 01 8333873

E-mail: info@iwa.ie
Website: www.iwa.ie

Marino Therapy Centre
Aims to provide counselling and treatment for eating distress and allied complications.
Address: 42 Malahide Road, Clontarf, Dublin 3
Tel: 01 8333126
Helpline number: 01 8333063 (Mon, Wed, Fri & Sunday 6.p.m.–8.p.m.)
E-mail: marinotherapy@gmail.com
Website: www.marinotherapycentre.com

Marriage and Relationship Counselling Services
Aims to provide marriage and relationship counselling.
Address: 38 Upper Fitzwilliam Street, Dublin 2
Tel: 1890 380380
E-mail: info@mrcs.ie
Website: www.mrcs.ie

Mater Dei Counselling Service
Aims to work with young people (12–18) and their families in relation to general adolescent problems.
Address: Clonliffe Road, Dublin 3
Tel: 01 8371892
Fax: 01 8372025
E-mail: materdei@teencounselling.com

Mental Health Ireland
Aims to promote positive mental health and to support those with mental illness and their families.
Address: Mensana House, 6 Adelaide St, Dun Laoghaire, Co. Dublin
Tel: 01 2841166
Fax: 01 2841736
E-mail: information@mentalhealthireland.ie
Website: www.mentalhealthireland.ie

National Children's Resource Centre
Aims to provide a library and information service on all aspects of childcare.
Address: Barnardos, Christchurch Square, Dublin 8
Tel: 01 4549699
Fax: 01 4530300
E-mail: ncrc@barnardos.ie
Website: www.barnardos.ie

Out and About Association (OANDA)
Aims to provide information to sufferers of agoraphobia, panic attacks and social anxiety disorders.
Address: 140 St Lawrence's Road, Clontarf, Dublin 3
Tel: 01 8338252
Fax: 01 8334243

Parentline
Aims to provide support for parents and guardians with family difficulties.
Address: Carmichael House, North Brunswick Street, Dublin 7
Tel: 01 8787230

Fax: 01 8735737
Helpline number: 1890 927277
E-mail: info@parentline.ie
Website: www.parentline.ie

Rainbows Ireland
Aims to help children and adults work through the grief of death or separation.
Address: Loreto Centre, Crumlin Road, Dublin 12
Tel: 01 4734175
Fax: 01 4734177
E-mail: ask@rainbowsireland.com
Website: www.rainbowsireland.com

Rutland Centre
Aims to provide residential treatment to people with a history of addiction in a variety of areas.
Address: Knocklyon House, Knocklyon Road, Templeogue, Dublin 16
Tel: 01 4946358
Fax: 01 4946444
E-mail: info@rutlandcentre.ie
Website: www.rutlandcentre.ie

The Samaritans
Aims to provide 24-hour support for people feeling distress, despair or suicidal feelings.
Address: 112 Marlborough Street, Dublin
Tel: 01 8727700
Helpline number:1850 609090
E-mail: jo@samaritans.org
Website: www.samaritans.org

Sólás
Aims to provide information and counselling to bereaved children and their families.
Address: Christchurch Square, Dublin 8
Tel: 01 4730355
Fax: 01 4530300
Helpline number: 01 4732110 (Mon–Fri 10a.m.–12noon)
E-mail: bereavement@barnardos.ie
Website: www.barnardos.ie

Schizophrenia Ireland
Aims to uphold the rights and needs of all those affected by schizophrenia and related illnesses and disorders.
Address: 38 Blessington Street Dublin 7
Tel: 01 8601620
Fax: 01 8601602
Helpline number: 1890 621631 (Mon–Fri 9a.m.–4p.m.)
E-mail: info@sirl.ie
Website: www.sirl.ie

Victim Support
Aims to provide practical advice and emotional support for victims of crime.
Address: Haliday House, 32 Arran Quay, Dublin 7.
Tel: 01 8780870
Fax: 01 8780944
Helpline number: 1850 661771
E-mail: info@victimsupport.ie
Website: www.victimsupport.ie

Index